❧ The Gift of Anger ❧

The Gift of Anger

And Other Lessons from
My Grandfather Mahatma Gandhi

ARUN GANDHI

MICHAEL JOSEPH
an imprint of
PENGUIN BOOKS

MICHAEL JOSEPH

UK | USA | Canada | Ireland | Australia
India | New Zealand | South Africa

Michael Joseph is part of the Penguin Random House group of companies
whose addresses can be found at global.penguinrandomhouse.com

First published in the United States of America by Gallery Books,
an imprint of Simon & Schuster 2017
First published in Great Britain by Michael Joseph 2017

001

Interior design by Jamie Putorti
Printed in Great Britain by Clays Ltd, St Ives plc
A CIP catalogue record for this book is available from the British Library

HARDBACK ISBN: 978–0–718–18750–7
OM PAPERBACK ISBN: 978–0–718–18751–4

www.greenpenguin.co.uk

MIX
Paper from
responsible sources
FSC
www.fsc.org   FSC® C018179

Penguin Random House is committed to a
sustainable future for our business, our readers
and our planet. This book is made from Forest
Stewardship Council® certified paper.

I dedicate this book to my four great grandchildren, Elizabeth (Ellie), Michael (Micah), Jonathan (Jonu), and Maya, and all the just-born and not-yet-born children of the world who must become the change if this world is to be saved from disaster.

· CONTENTS ·

❧ The Gift of Anger ❧

Lessons from My Grandfather

We were going to visit Grandfather. To me, he was not the great Mahatma Gandhi whom the world revered but just "Bapuji," the kindly grandfather my parents talked about often. Coming to visit him in India from our home in South Africa required a long journey. We had just endured a sixteen-hour trip on a crowded train from Mumbai, packed into a third-class compartment that reeked of cigarettes and sweat and the smoke from the steam engine. We were all tired as the train chugged into the Wardha station and it felt good to escape the coal dust and step onto the platform and gulp fresh air.

It was barely nine in the morning, but the early sun was blazing hot. The station was just a platform with a single room for the stationmaster, but my dad found a porter in a long red shirt and loincloth to help us with our bags and lead us to where the horse buggies (called *tongas* in India) were waiting. Dad lifted Ela, my six-year-old sister, onto the buggy and asked me to get in next to her. He and Mom would walk behind.

"Then I'll walk too," I said.

"It's a long distance—probably eight miles," Dad pointed out.

"That is not a problem for me," I insisted. I was twelve years old and wanted to appear tough.

It didn't take long to regret my decision. The sun kept getting hotter, and the road was paved for only about a mile from the station. Before long I was tired and sweat-soaked and covered with dust and grime, but I knew that I couldn't climb into the buggy now. At home the rule was that if you said something, you had to back it up with action. It didn't matter if my ego was stronger than my legs—I had to keep going.

Finally we approached Bapuji's ashram, called Sevagram. After all our travels, we had reached a remote spot, in the poorest of the poor heartland of India. I had heard so much about the beauty and love Grandfather brought to the world that I might have expected blossoming flowers and flowing waterfalls. Instead the place appeared flat, dry, dusty, and unremarkable, with some mud huts around an open common space. Had I come so far for this barren, unimpressive spot? I thought there might be at least a welcome party to greet us, but nobody seemed to pay any attention to our arrival. "Where is everybody?" I asked my mom.

We went to a simple hut where I took a bath and scrubbed my face. I had met Bapuji once before, when I was five years old, but I didn't remember the visit, and I was slightly nervous now for our second meeting. My parents had told us to be on good behavior when greeting Grandfather because he was an important man. Even in South Africa I heard people speaking reverentially about him, and I imagined that somewhere on the grounds of the ashram was the mansion where Bapuji lived, surrounded by a swarm of attendants.

Instead I was shocked when we walked to another simple hut and stepped across a mud-floor veranda into a room no more than ten by fourteen feet. There was Bapuji, squatting in a corner of the floor on a thin cotton mattress.

Later I would learn that visiting heads of state squatted on mats next to him to talk and consult with the great Gandhi. But now Bapuji gave us his beautiful, toothless smile and beckoned us forward.

Following our parents' lead, my sister and I went to bow at his feet in traditional Indian obeisance. He would have none of that, quickly pulling us to him to give us affectionate hugs. He kissed us on both cheeks, and Ela squealed with surprise and delight.

"How was your journey?" Bapuji asked.

I was so overawed that I stuttered, "Bapuji, I walked all the way from the station."

He laughed and I saw a twinkle in his eye. "Is that so? I am so proud of you," he said, and planted more kisses on my cheeks.

I could immediately feel his unconditional love, and that to me was all the blessing I needed.

But there were many more blessings to come.

My parents and Ela stayed just a few days at the ashram before heading off to visit my mother's large family in other parts of India. But I was to live and travel with Bapuji for the next two years, as I grew from a naïve child of twelve to a wiser young man of fourteen. In that time I learned from him lessons that forever changed the direction of my life.

Bapuji often had a spinning wheel at his side, and I like to think of his life as a golden thread of stories and lessons that continue to weave in and out through the generations, making a stronger fabric for all our lives. Many people now know my grandfather only from the movies, or they remember that he started the nonviolence movements that eventually came to the United States and helped bring about civil rights. But I knew him as a warm, loving grandfather who looked for the best in me—and so brought it out. He inspired me and so many others to be better than we ever imagined we could be. He cared about political justice not from some grand theoretical view but because he was moved by the plight of each individual. He thought each of us deserved to live the best life we possibly could.

We all need Bapuji's lessons now, more than ever. My grandfather would be sad at the depth of anger in the world today. But he would not despair.

──────── ✿✿✿ ────────

All humanity is one family.

──────────────────────

"All humanity is one family," he told me time and again. He faced dangers and hatred in his time, but his practical philosophy of nonviolence helped liberate India and was the model for the advancement of rights around the world.

Now, again, we have to stop fighting each other to effectively address the real dangers we face. Mass shootings and lethal bombings have become part of our daily reality in America. We have seen policemen and peaceful protesters killed in cold blood. Children are murdered in schools and in our streets, and social media has become a forum for hate and prejudice. Politicians incite violence and anger rather than seek common ground.

My grandfather's example of nonviolence was never meant to be passivity or weakness. In fact he saw non-violence as a way to make yourself morally and ethically stronger and more able to move toward the goal of bring-ing harmony to society. When he was just getting under way with his nonviolence campaigns, he asked people to help him find a name for his new movement, and one of his cousins suggested the Sanskrit word *sadagraha*, which means "firmness in a good cause." Bapuji liked the word but decided to modify it slightly to *satyagraha*, or "firmness for truth." Later, people sometimes translated it as "soul force," which powerfully reminds us that real strength comes from having the right values as we seek social transformation.

What I see us all needing right now is a return to my grandfather's *satyagraha*, or soul force. He created a movement that led to huge political upheaval and brought self-rule to hundreds of millions of Indians. But most important, Bapuji tried to show that we can achieve our goals through love and truth and that the greatest advances occur when we give up our distrust and look for strength in positivity and courage.

My grandfather did not believe in labels or divisions between people, and though he was deeply spiritual, he objected to religion when it divided rather than connected people. On the ashram we awoke at 4:30 every morning to get ready for 5 a.m. prayers. Bapuji had read the texts of all religions, and the universalist prayers he offered were taken from all of them. He believed that every religion has a bit of truth—and that trouble occurs when we think that one bit is the whole and only truth.

Bapuji spoke out against British rule in favor of self-determination for all people, and for that this man who wanted only to spread love and peace spent nearly six years in Indian jails. His ideas of peace and unity were so threatening to many that he, his wife, and his best friend and confidant, Mahadev Desai, were all imprisoned. Desai had a heart attack and died in jail in 1942, and Grandfather's beloved wife, Kasturbai, finally failed on February 22, 1944, with her head resting in his lap. Three months after her death, Grandfather emerged from prison, the sole survivor. The following year he took me in and made it his mission to teach me how to have a better life.

The two years that I lived with Bapuji were an important time for both of us. While I was with him, his work for an independent India reached fruition, but the violence and partition that came with it were not part of his dream. As he made changes on the world stage, I learned to make changes in myself, overcoming my own, often unwieldy emotions and discovering how to fulfill my potential and see the world through new eyes. I got to witness history at the same time that Bapuji offered me simple, practical lessons in reaching my personal goals. It was an intensive course in his philosophy "Be the change you wish to see in the world."

———————— ❀ ❀ ❀ ————————

Be the change you wish to see in the world.

We need that change right now, as we reach intolerable levels of violence and hatred in the world. People are desperate for change but feel helpless. A drastic economic imbalance means more than 15 million children in America and hundreds of millions around the world often don't have enough to eat, while those who live with abundance feel they have a license to waste. When right-wing fascists recently defaced a statue of my grandfather in a town square in northern India, they promised, "You will witness a trail of terror." We must transform our own lives if we want to end this madness.

My grandfather feared this very moment in our history. A reporter asked him just one week before he was murdered, "What do you think will happen with your philosophy after you die?" He replied with great sadness, "The people will follow me in life, worship me in death, but not make my cause their cause." We must once again make his cause ours. His daily wisdom can help us solve the problems we still face today. We have never needed my grandfather more than at this very moment.

Bapuji used transcendent truths and practical guidance to change the course of history. Now it is time for us all to use them.

The lessons I learned from Bapuji transformed my life, and I hope they will help you find greater peace and meaning in yours.

Use Anger for Good

My grandfather amazed the world by responding to violence and hatred with love and forgiveness. He never fell prey to the toxicity of anger. I was not so successful. As an Indian child growing up in racially charged South Africa, I was attacked by white children for not being white enough and black children for not being black.

I remember walking to buy candy one Saturday afternoon in a white neighborhood when three teenage boys pounced on me. One slapped me across the face, and when I fell, the other two started kicking me and laughing. They ran away before anyone could catch them. I was just nine years old. The next year, during the Hindu Festival of Lights, my family was in town rejoicing with friends. Heading to one of their homes, I passed a group of young black African men hanging out on the street corner. One of them reached over and whacked me hard across the back with a stick for no reason other than that I was Indian. I seethed with fury and wanted to retaliate.

I began weightlifting with some vague idea that I would become strong enough to get my revenge. My parents, who saw themselves as ambassadors of Bapuji's teachings of nonviolence, despaired that I got into so many fights. They tried to make me less aggressive, but they couldn't do much about my rage.

I wasn't happy about being angry all the time. Holding grudges and fantasizing about getting even made me feel weaker, not stronger. My parents hoped that my staying at the ashram with Bapuji would help me understand my inner fury and be better able to cope with it. I too hoped so.

In my first meetings with my grandfather, I was struck that he always seemed calm and in control, no matter what anyone said or did. I promised myself that I would follow his example, and I didn't do badly for a while. After my parents and sister left, I met some boys my age who lived in the village down the road, and we started to play together. They had an old tennis ball they used for a soccer ball, and I put a couple of stones in place for the goals.

I loved playing soccer. Even though the kids made fun of my South African accent from the very first day, I had dealt with worse, so I tolerated their ribbing. But in the midst of one fast-moving game, one of the boys purposely tripped me as I chased after the ball. I fell to the hard and dusty ground. My ego was as badly bruised as my knee—and I felt a familiar rush of anger, my heart beating hard in my chest and my mind wanting revenge. I grabbed a rock. Getting up off the ground, furious, I raised my arm to throw the rock as hard as I could at the offender.

But a small voice in my head said, "Don't do it."

I threw the rock to the ground and ran back to the ashram. With tears streaming down my cheeks, I found my grandfather and told him the story.

"I am angry all the time, Bapuji. I don't know what to do."

I had let him down and thought he would be unhappy with me. But he patted me soothingly on the back and said, "Get your spinning wheel and let us both spin some cotton."

My grandfather had taught me how to use a spinning wheel as soon as I arrived at the ashram. I did it every day for an hour in the morning and an hour in the evening; it was very calming. Bapuji liked to multitask even before anybody used that word. He would often say, "While sitting and speaking, we can use our hands to spin." Now I got the little machine and set it up.

Bapuji smiled and prepared to spin a lesson along with the cotton.

"I want to tell you a story," he said, as I took my place next to him. "There once was a boy your age. He was always angry because nothing seemed to happen his way. He couldn't recognize the value of other people's perspectives, and so when people provoked him, he responded with angry outbursts."

I suspected the boy was me, so I kept spinning and listened even more intently.

"One day he got into a very serious fight and accidentally committed murder," he continued. "In one moment of thoughtless passion he destroyed his own life by taking the life of someone else."

"I promise, Bapuji, I'll be better." I hadn't the faintest idea *how* to be better, but I didn't want my anger to kill someone.

Bapuji nodded. "You do have a lot of rage," he said. "Your parents told me about all the fights you have been in at home."

"I'm so sorry," I said, afraid that I would start to cry again.

But Bapuji had planned a different moral than I expected. He looked over at me from behind his spinning wheel. "I am glad to see you can be moved to anger.

Anger is good. I get angry all the time," he confessed as his fingers turned the wheel.

I could not believe what I was hearing. "I have never seen you angry," I replied.

"Because I have learned to use my anger for good," he explained. "Anger to people is like gas to the automobile—it fuels you to move forward and get to a better place. Without it, we would not be motivated to rise to a challenge. It is an energy that compels us to define what is just and unjust."

———— ❀❀❀ ————

Use your anger for good. Anger to people is like gas to the automobile—it fuels you to move forward and get to a better place. Without it, we would not be motivated to rise to a challenge. It is an energy that compels us to define what is just and unjust.

Grandfather explained that when he was a boy in South Africa, he too had suffered from violent prejudice, and it made him angry. But eventually he learned that it didn't help to seek vengeance, and he began to fight against prejudice and discrimination with compassion, responding to anger and hate with goodness. He believed in the power of truth and love. Seeking revenge made no sense to him. An eye for an eye only makes the whole world blind.

I was surprised to learn that Bapuji hadn't been born even-tempered. Now he was revered and called by the honorific *Mahatma*, but once he was just an unruly kid. When he was my age, he stole money from his parents to buy cigarettes and got into trouble with other kids. After an arranged marriage with my grandmother when they were both just thirteen years old, he sometimes shouted at her, and once, after an argument, he tried to physically throw her out of the house. But he didn't like the person he was becoming, so he began to mold himself into the even-tempered, well-controlled person he wanted to be.

"So I could learn to do that?" I asked.

"You are doing it right now," he said with a smile.

As we both sat at our spinning wheels, I tried to let it sink in that anger could be used for good. I might still *feel* anger, but I could learn to channel it to positive ends—like the political changes Grandfather calmly pursued in South Africa and India.

Bapuji explained that our spinning wheels themselves were an example of how anger could create positive change. Producing cloth had been a cottage industry in India for centuries, but now the big textile mills in Great Britain were taking cotton from India, processing it, and selling it back to Indians at high prices. The people were angry; they were in rags because they couldn't afford to buy British-made cloth. But instead of attacking the British industry for impoverishing people, Bapuji himself began spinning as a way of encouraging every family to have their own wheel and be self-sufficient. It had a huge impact all across the country and in England.

Bapuji saw that I was listening intently, so he offered another analogy—he did love analogies!—comparing anger to electricity. "When we channel electricity intelligently, we can use it to improve our life, but if we abuse it, we could die. So as with electricity, we must learn to use anger wisely for the good of humanity."

When we channel electricity intelligently, we can use
it to improve our life, but if we abuse it, we could
die. So as with electricity, we must learn to use anger
wisely for the good of humanity.

I didn't want my anger to short-circuit my life or anyone else's. But how could I make it a spark for change?

Bapuji was deeply spiritual, but he could be practical too. He gave me a notebook and a pencil and told me that I should use them to keep an anger journal. "Every time you feel great anger, stop and write down who or what caused your feelings and why you reacted so angrily," he instructed. "The goal is to get to the root of the anger. Only when you understand the source can you find a solution."

The key, Bapuji explained, was acknowledging everyone's point of view. An anger journal wasn't just a way to spew anger and feel righteous, as too many people do now. (Then they reread the journal and feel angry and justified all over again!) Instead an anger journal should be a way of trying to understand what caused the conflict and how it can be resolved. I needed to detach myself and see the other person's side. This wasn't a prescription for giving in to the other person, but rather a technique for finding a solution that didn't lead to more anger and resentment.

Sometimes we think we want to resolve conflicts, but our methods just make things worse. We turn angry and intimidating, thinking we will make people do what we want. But attacks and criticism and threats of punishment backfire with both children and adults. Our angry responses cause the battles to escalate. We become bullies, not realizing that bullies ultimately aren't powerful at all. Those who display meanness and a berating style on the playground, in business, or in political campaigns are usually the weakest and most insecure. Bapuji taught me that being able to understand another's viewpoint and forgive is the sign of real strength.

Bapuji explained that we spend a lot of time building strong and healthy bodies but not enough time building a strong and healthy mind. If our mind isn't under our control, we get angry and snap and say or do something we later regret. There are probably dozens of times in each day when we feel that surge of anger or frustration and have to decide how to respond. A colleague at work says something, and we give a snippy reply, or we get an irritating e-mail and fire back without thinking. We even let our anger hurt the people we love the most, our children or spouse. They disappoint us or say something we disagree with, and we lash out.

Our words can irreparably hurt the people we should be treating with kindness and love—and we don't realize that the anger is hurting us too. Think how miserable you feel when you're being insulting or cruel to someone. Your body tenses and your mind feels like it's on fire. You get consumed by your outburst and can't focus on anything else. Anger narrows your world so that all you can see is the insult of the moment. Maybe later you calm down and go back to apologize, but the harm is already done. When we react rashly and lash out, it's as if we have shot bullets that can't be put back in the gun.

We have to remember that we have the option to react differently.

That day at the spinning wheel, Bapuji told me about the need to treat anger as a warning that something is wrong. Writing in the journal was just a first step. Gaining control over my mind would ensure that I could respond properly in the future. Instead of saying something you don't mean or inflicting emotional harm on others, Grandfather explained, you can focus on a solution that will make everyone happy. If your immediate response didn't help, what reaction might bring better understanding?

"I need to strengthen my mind, Bapuji!" I said. "What kind of exercises do I need to do?"

He told me to start very simply. I should sit in a quiet room without any distractions (these days that would mean no cell phone!) and hold something lovely, like a flower or a photograph of a flower, in front of me. I should concentrate fully on the object for a minute or more, then close my eyes and see how long I could hold the image in my mind. In the beginning the image might vanish almost as soon as I closed my eyes. But if I did it regularly, I would be able to hold the image longer and longer. That showed I was pushing out distractions and gaining control over my mind.

When you grow up, he told me, you can go to the second stage of the exercise. In that same quiet room, close your eyes and let yourself be aware only of how you are breathing in and out. Try to focus your mind completely on your breathing and keep extraneous thoughts away. These exercises will give you greater control over your responses, he said, so that in a moment of crisis you will not act rashly.

I started doing Bapuji's exercise the next day— and I still do it faithfully. It remains the best way I know to control my mind. It took me some months to learn how to channel my anger into intelligent action, but eventually I did succeed. This kind of anger management is a lifelong exercise. You cannot do it for a few months and think you have mastered it. Circumstances in life change, and along with it the triggers that cause anger also change. So it is important to be constantly vigilant and prepared to deal with any curveball thrown at us.

I was curious to know how my grandfather first learned about anger being used for good. "Bapuji, can I ask you a question?"

"Of course you may, Arun," he responded.

"How did you learn about anger being so useful and powerful?"

He stopped spinning and laughed out loud. "It was your grandmother who taught me this lesson."

"Really? How? What happened?"

"I was married so young and I didn't know how to behave with a wife. After school I would go to the library to find books on marital relationships. We had one argument where I was shouting and she responded calmly and rationally. I was speechless. Later I thought about this episode and realized how irrational we get when angry and how beautifully your grandmother defused the situation. If she had retorted angrily we would have had a shouting match, and who knows where that would have ended? The more I thought about it, the more I was convinced that we must all learn how to use anger intelligently."

My grandmother had recently died in jail, sent there with Bapuji for civil disobedience, and I knew how much he missed her. He held a prayer service every month in her memory. His story made me realize how powerful it is to respond calmly when someone is angry. It's unusual too. More often, when one person starts shouting, the other person gets defensive and shouts back, raising the level of anger higher and higher. But if you can speak kindly to the people who hurt you or made you angry, the moment gets turned on its head.

I understood that lesson in a theoretical way when Bapuji taught it to me, but it became real only years later, as the result of a situation that brought all my emotions to a boil. At age twenty-two, living in South Africa again, I returned to India to visit relatives. As I was planning to go back home and continue the fight against discrimination and apartheid, I got acute appendicitis and needed immediate surgery. The nurse who admitted me, Sunanda Ambegaonkar, was both kind and beautiful, and in the five days I was in hospital she completely captured my heart. We were both very shy, and it took me a long time to convince her to go with me to a movie. I arrived at the theater at 3 p.m. and waited and waited. And waited. She finally arrived just before 6 p.m., not expecting to find me there. She claimed a medical emergency delayed her, but later she admitted she had simply suffered from cold feet.

After that rocky start, we fell in love and got married. Sunanda needed a visa to return with me to South Africa, but I didn't anticipate any problem. Since I was a citizen of the country, I should have had the right to bring my spouse with me. But those were the days of rigid apartheid, and she wasn't welcome. For more than a year we did everything we could to persuade the government to let us return—but we got nowhere. She couldn't come with me. I had to choose between being with my bride in India and being with my widowed mother and sisters in South Africa. I was angry and distraught. How could a government cause such unnecessary grief? The decision was heartrending, but I chose to stay with my adored new wife and live in India.

About ten years later a good friend of mine came to India to visit. When I met his ship, a white man grabbed my hand and said he was going to be in Mumbai for almost a week and was eager to see the city. Since I was the first Indian he had encountered, might I be able to help? He introduced himself as Jackie Basson, a member of Parliament in South Africa.

I felt the old fury rising in me. His government had insulted me and refused to let me return. I didn't want to help him—I wanted to throw him overboard and get my revenge. But by then I'd had some practice in Bapuji's lessons on channeling anger intelligently, so I swallowed hard and decided not to act rashly. I shook hands with him and explained politely that I was a victim of apartheid, forced to be in India because his government wouldn't let my dear wife return with me.

"I disagree with what your government is doing," I told him. "However, you are a guest in this city and I am going to ensure that you have a pleasant stay."

First I got my good friend settled; then, for the next several days, my wife and I took Mr. and Mrs. Basson around Mumbai, treating them warmly and showing them the sights. We talked about apartheid and how it had pulled our family apart. On the last day, we said good-bye—and both of them began weeping.

"You have opened our eyes to the evils of prejudice," Basson said, embracing me. "The government I have supported is wrong. We will go back and fight apartheid."

As I watched them board the ship, I was dubious that our few days together had really changed his position. "I'm not sure how sincere he is," I said to my wife. "Let's wait and see what happens."

I didn't have to wait long. The moment Basson got back home, he began speaking out against apartheid. He was so ardent in his opposition that the ruling party threw him out and he lost the next election. But he remained steadfast, and his strength no doubt helped persuade others.

Observing his incredible change confirmed for me the power of Bapuji's philosophy of using anger intelligently. If I had snapped at Basson (or thrown him overboard), as I wanted to when we first met, I would have had some momentary satisfaction. I'd have rebuked a government official—and he deserved it! But the end result wouldn't have been satisfying at all. He would have gone back home more convinced than ever that racism was the correct position and that he should stay away from blacks and Indians.

Using anger intelligently makes life better on a personal basis and a global one too. Grandfather discovered that early in his political experience. Back in 1913, when he lived in South Africa, he wanted to launch another campaign against the prejudice and segregation there. He made a friendly request to the government for a dialogue, making sure he didn't use any aggressive or accusatory language. When the government failed to respond, he let the public know that he was seeking a peaceful solution and had no aggressive intentions, and he asked the people to join him in civil protests.

At about the same time, the workers of South African Railways announced they were going to strike for better working conditions. Grandfather realized this would be a huge inconvenience and dominate everyone's attention, so he decided to suspend his campaign until the strike ended.

"You should join us," one leader suggested. "Let's join forces. A strike is a legitimate nonviolent campaign, and we are fighting a common enemy."

"I don't consider anyone to be my enemy," Grandfather replied. "They are all my friends. I want to educate them and change their hearts."

The workers struck as planned and went out into the streets, shouting angry slogans. They were furious and frustrated and easily incited to violence, which gave the police justification for using excessive force to battle them and crush the strike. In about four days the workers had to go back to work without gaining anything.

Shortly after, Bapuji launched his campaign against discrimination. He set a tone of quiet protest without anger. In spite of police atrocities, he never referred to the police or the administration as enemies. His idea was to win the sympathy of everyone—including the police—not to hurt or embarrass them. When the police came to make arrests, Bapuji and his followers quietly submitted, calmly stepping into the police vans. Other protesters took their place, and they too were taken away. This continued until, after two weeks, the prisons were so full they could not accommodate another person. The prime minister, General Jan C. Smuts, then invited Grandfather to discuss a settlement. When they sat down together, Smuts confessed that he did not know how to deal with Grandfather and his followers: "You are always so respectful, kind, and considerate that it is hard to crush you with violence. It was much easier to attack the strikers who displayed so much anger."

Being calm in the face of anger isn't always easy, but once you try it and see the results, you will believe in it. You don't have to wait for a major event or protest; it's a method we can all try on a daily basis with the people closest to us. As we change our own abilities to channel anger, we will see changes in the people around us. Nobody wants to be bullied; we would all rather be understood and appreciated. Letting anger motivate us to correct wrongs has great value, but only when our real goal is to seek a solution and not just prove that we are right.

As we sat at our spinning wheels that day at the ashram, Bapuji hugged me and hoped that I understood his lesson. "Use your anger wisely," he told me. "Let it help you find solutions of love and truth."

Use your anger wisely. Let it help you find solutions of love and truth.

I felt Bapuji's love very deeply, and from that moment I understood that love and kindness are stronger than anger. I would continue to face injustice and prejudice my whole life, but I would never again feel I had to throw a rock. I could find other solutions.

Don't Be Afraid to Speak Up

Although Grandfather hoped that those who joined him in the ashram were doing so to pursue the higher Truth, there were many who simply joined him as groupies. He tried to make all of us think for ourselves. He believed that you shouldn't try to please others at a cost to yourself, and he didn't mind if his followers challenged him.

"A 'no' uttered from the deepest conviction is better than a 'yes' merely uttered to please, or worse, to avoid trouble," he told us. But it was still hard for most people to question him. He was seen as wise and saintly, and the people who came to the ashram wanted to learn from him.

※ ※ ※

A "no" uttered from the deepest conviction is better than a "yes" merely uttered to please, or worse, to avoid trouble.

It took my six-year-old sister, Ela, to prove to everyone that speaking up for what you want is not only okay but really important.

When we first arrived at Sevagram, my parents and Ela stayed with me for a week. Ela and I were used to our life at home in South Africa, where we lived on the Phoenix ashram, which Bapuji had also started. It was his first experiment in communal living. At the beginning only our immediate relatives and a few cousins lived there, but soon friends joined, then people who were intrigued by the concept of living in cooperation with each other and nature.

Life at the Phoenix ashram was very simple, but it seemed almost opulent compared to life at Sevagram. At home we had functional furniture and lived in houses of wood and corrugated metal; here it was all mud huts and sitting on the floor. But the biggest difference was the food. At both ashrams we raised crops and ate what we grew, but at Phoenix my mother cooked it into meals with great variety and many spices. The food at Sevagram was (to put it plainly) terrible. Every day we got some version of boiled, unsalted pumpkin. Every meal was as boring and tasteless as the one before. Boiled pumpkin for breakfast, lunch, and dinner. Ela and I complained to our parents, but they hushed us, pointing out that we were guests and needed to follow Bapuji's plan. We tried talking to the people who worked in the kitchen, but they told us the same thing: "We are following what Gandhi wants." Everyone assumed that he had decreed the menu, and so there must be a reason for it. We weren't the only ones who would have liked a different vegetable now and then, but since no one wanted to appear insolent, no one felt comfortable questioning what we ate.

Little Ela had no such compunctions. Toward the end of a week of eating pumpkin, she'd had enough. With all the righteous anger of a six-year-old, she marched into Bapuji's mud hut. "You should change the name of this place to Kola ashram!" she declared, using the Indian word for *pumpkin*.

Astounded by this outburst, Bapuji looked up from his work and asked, "What do you mean, my child?"

"Ever since we came here we get nothing but pumpkin to eat, morning, noon, and night. I am sick of it," she blurted out.

"Is that so?" Bapuji was genuinely astonished. But he had a sense of humor, so he added, "We must look into it. If what you say is right, then we must indeed change the name."

For himself, Bapuji ate the barest amount necessary for nutrition and often used fasting as a form of nonviolent protest. But he did not expect everyone to follow his stringent and meticulous diet. He was very busy and seldom attended the communal meals, so he hadn't even known what we were eating.

That evening after the prayer service, when he usually delivered his sermon, he asked the manager of the ashram to explain why everyone was made to eat pumpkin every day. Munna Lal, the manager, asserted that he was trying to follow Grandfather's instructions to eat only what was grown on the farm.

"Are you saying that our farm can produce only pumpkin?" Bapuji asked.

"You said we should eat simply, so I thought that's what you wanted."

"*Simple* doesn't mean you have to eat the same thing all the time."

The manager looked abashed. "We planted a whole field of pumpkins, and we have such a bumper crop that we do not know what to do with them all. That is why we've been cooking so much pumpkin," he confessed.

Bapuji said that wasn't very good planning. "We should grow a variety of fruits and vegetables but prepare simple meals." But he never admonished without a solution. "Now since you have a surplus of pumpkins, please take them to the village and barter them for other vegetables."

Ela was the hero of the day—and not just because the food improved so quickly. Bapuji used her confronting him as a lesson that we should never stop speaking out against problems. How can we create change in the world if we are afraid to say what is wrong?

৪ঃঃ

After Ela and my parents left, I quickly fell into the rhythm of the ashram. Every day I woke up at 4:30 and got ready for the 5 a.m. prayers. Bapuji led the prayers and then spoke to all of us who had gathered about important issues of the day. Sometimes, though, he just addressed practical topics for the ashram, and I would smile to myself, thinking how surprised the world would be to hear the great Gandhi discussing the best way to water vegetables. He never thought any subject was beneath him.

Afterward I exercised for an hour, including some yoga, and then came daily chores. We all had to help with even the most unpleasant duties, like cleaning the toilets. In almost every other place in India, menial tasks were done by only the lowliest castes. But Bapuji believed that breaking down distinctions between people would help end prejudice in the world, so each of us took a turn at the dreariest jobs. Carrying away waste in buckets to be used as compost was the worst for me. At the beginning I scrunched up my nose at the smell and hoped that as Gandhi's grandson, I might get special treatment. But not a chance! Everyone worked together, and after a while the job didn't seem so bad. Bapuji's teaching that everyone was equal made you look at work in a different way.

After chores it was time for breakfast (at last!), and after that I would go outside with my tutor to do my lessons in the blazing sun. The temperature sometimes soared past 115 degrees Fahrenheit, but getting out of the sun wasn't an option because my eccentric tutor had taken a vow not to seek shelter, though sometimes I was allowed to drape a cotton towel over my head. People on the ashram often took vows as a way of showing mental discipline and the capacity to follow through on their plans—though I would have been happier on those hot days if my tutor was a little less strict in following his vow.

Taking vows was also a common practice in the Hindu tradition. Once, when I was visiting my maternal grandmother, one of my aunts took a vow to eat only two meals a day. We were all together on a picnic, and my sister and I noticed that she didn't eat lunch but kept munching all afternoon on small candies. We asked her why. "I've already eaten breakfast, and now I'm stretching out that one meal until it's time for dinner!" she explained.

Unlike my aunt, my tutor was stricter with his vows and didn't cut any corners, so we spent all day outside, with just a half-hour break for lunch. In addition to the heat, it was usually dusty and dry, and when the rains came, the whole place turned into a mud bath. Then came the other extreme, as temperatures in winter plunged to 30 degrees.

Taking a no-shelter vow wasn't my tutor's only quirk. He'd once had an argument with another resident and started shouting at him. The matter went to Bapuji, who pointed out to my tutor that he'd said some awful things and needed to learn to control his anger.

"What do you think I should do?" the tutor asked.

"You're an intelligent man. I'll leave it to you to decide," Bapuji answered.

My tutor shocked everyone, including my grandfather, by finding a piece of metal wire and literally sewing his lips together. He wrote a note explaining that his lips would remain sewn shut until he was sure that he wouldn't lose his temper again. He took a long time convincing himself, and for months he ate only liquids poured into the side of his mouth through a funnel. When I met him, the scars on his upper and lower lips were still fresh. So it wasn't likely he was going to run under a tree because of a little heat.

Bapuji was comfortable with eccentricity and having your own point of view. But he became exasperated by people who gave up reasoning and stopped thinking for themselves. He would probably be unhappy to find that the habit of following the crowd has only gotten worse as social media lets us "like" and "follow" each other without much thought. A celebrity describes her weight-loss regimen and millions of people try it, even if it makes as little sense as the pumpkin diet. A politician makes rude or bigoted statements and people don't object because they support the same political party. Religious leaders make pronouncements that deny women's rights and people accept them without a murmur in the name of tradition.

Many politicians now follow opinion polls before taking a stand on issues and speak out only when it will serve their own interests. They rarely stop to listen to others' viewpoints because they fear that if they change their opinion they will get pummeled by the press for "flip-flopping." Bapuji didn't care about party politics or always needing to be right. He confided to me that he tested new ideas every day and constantly questioned those he held dear. He wouldn't let himself get complacent. He knew that when you follow any teaching rigidly and dogmatically, you make a mockery of it and undermine its true purpose.

I think Bapuji would have a few things to say to people who aren't willing to think for themselves and speak out against wrong. Six-year-old Ela could do it, and the rest of us should too. We can't let ourselves be swept along by others' visions without stopping to decide if they make sense to our own beliefs. If you are accepting someone else's definition of *right* or *good* and not working to find what you value in yourself, then you are accepting boiled, unsalted pumpkin.

You prove your strength when you find what matters most deeply to you and are willing to stand up for it, even if the tide seems to be going in a different direction.

❦✢❧

As Gandhi's grandson, I have tried to emulate his example of nonviolence and understanding throughout my life. For a while I thought I needed to hew exactly to his path and never deviate. But then I remembered how proud he was when Ela spoke up, and I realized that he would want me to think for myself. He believed in a living philosophy that was always being tested and perfected. I'm not the same person as Bapuji—all you have to do is look at me to know that.

"You are so big and fat and your grandfather was so lean," kids would say, teasing me, when I returned from India.

Teenagers are always insecure, and being compared to the great Gandhi sometimes seemed more than I could bear.

"How can I live with this legacy?" I asked my mother once.

"If the legacy is a burden, it will get heavy," she told me wisely. "If it's a path to meaning and truth, it will feel much lighter."

After that I ignored the negative comments. I could admire my grandfather and want to further the causes he believed in, but I could still be my own person. Unlike Bapuji, I am not a vegetarian. I tried it but decided not to make it part of my life. I've had people come up to me when I was eating dinner at a restaurant as if it were a great "gotcha" moment. They knew I wanted to spread my grandfather's words, but I had a hamburger in front of me! I would try to explain that Bapuji did not believe you need to sign on to an entire dogma and surrender all sense of yourself. You need to think and question and make yourself part of the process. Rather than betraying my grandfather and his great causes, I am making his philosophy my own.

I learned from Bapuji that you should not live in a particular way only to please others. Following the crowd is no way to create change and improve the world. I often encounter people who work in big companies and stay at their desks late every night because they think it's what's expected. Are they really adding value—or are there ways they could be true to themselves and their own families and still get their work done? We have to be careful about following a path that doesn't make us happy because someone tells us it's right.

Many of us get caught up in materialistic pursuits because those are the images that get reinforced all around us through advertising, television, films, and social media. On some level we know that getting a bigger house or a faster car won't be the solution that makes us happier, but we have trouble refusing common expectations and saying, "I want something else."

Bapuji lived his life in absolute simplicity because he didn't think one person deserves more than another. When he was younger, however, he didn't accept that. While practicing law in London, he had a fancy suit made to order on Bond Street so that he would fit in. He even took dancing lessons and bought a violin to try to be a proper English gentleman.

Later, he moved to do law work in South Africa, and for one case, he needed to travel to Pretoria on an overnight train. He entered the first-class compartment with the appropriate ticket, but a tall, rugged white man protested his being there.

"Get out, you coolie," the man shouted, using the racial slur of the time.

"I have a valid first-class ticket," my grandfather replied.

"I don't care what you have. If you don't get off, I'm calling the police."

"That is your privilege" was my grandfather's response.

He sat calmly, unwilling to go to the third-class section for nonwhites.

The man left the train and returned with a policeman and a railway official, and the three of them literally threw Grandfather off the train. With smirks on their faces, they pitched his bags after him and signaled for the train to go on.

My grandfather sat overnight on the cold station platform, shivering and thinking about what he wanted to do.

"It has always been a mystery to me how men can feel themselves honored by the humiliation of their fellow beings," he wrote later.

───── ❀ ❀ ❀ ─────

It has always been a mystery to me how men can feel themselves honored by the humiliation of their fellow beings.

That long night on the platform might have been the start of Bapuji's realization that you have to speak up for what you believe. Acceding to other people's expectations doesn't make you happy or whole—and doesn't make the world any better. It was just a few days after this incident that he began to speak out against racial prejudice in a way that inspired people to respond. He began writing about the plight of Indians in South Africa and condemned the state's prejudicial policies.

By the time he returned to South Africa a few years later, my grandfather was already known for his strong position against apartheid. He sailed into the harbor along with two shiploads of Indian laborers. The government knew there would be trouble since the whites wanted to keep out immigrants and were furious at my grandfather for supporting the rights of all people. The government didn't let anybody disembark for nearly two weeks. When my grandfather finally got off the ship, a mob attacked him, beating him savagely until blood was streaming from his head. He could easily have been killed, but he made his way to the home of a friend, where his wife and sons (including my father) were waiting for him. He knew that speaking out against wrongs could be dangerous, but at that moment he decided that would never stop him. The pain of the encounter mattered less than the greater purpose.

One additional twist to that story occurred after the police arrested a few of the men who led the attack on my grandfather. The police asked Bapuji to file a complaint so they could press charges. He declined.

"I'll have to release them then," said the surprised police chief.

"That's fine," my grandfather replied.

He had decided that if he helped put them in jail, he was as guilty of perpetuating hatred as they were. Maybe hearing that he didn't believe in violence or revenge would make them rethink their own actions. Sometimes you speak loudest by not yelling.

When he moved back to India, Bapuji began wearing a cotton loincloth and a shawl over his shoulders rather than a shirt and trousers because, he said, he had no right to possess any more than the poorest in India. He didn't glorify poverty, and he wasn't naïve about money; he collected as much as he could whenever he traveled to give to those who needed it. But he understood the difference between the basic needs that make a difference in people's lives and the extravagance that doesn't.

My parents followed Bapuji's philosophy, and when I was young, they encouraged me to play with the children of the very poor black farm laborers who lived near our Phoenix ashram. It was one way to speak out against economic distinctions and help me put wealth in perspective. The kids didn't have any toys, but we would scrounge together to find matchboxes and shirt buttons and would glue them together to build miniature cars. Down at the nearby stream, we dug up black clay soil and molded figurines. We had fun creating things, and we cherished the toys we made. Today many kids get new plastic gadgets all the time, and they're tired of them in a day or two.

My parents believed that playtime should be constructive, so when I started school I taught my farm friends the ABCs and how to count. As soon as I could read, I taught them too. I was opening a whole new world to them, and they couldn't wait for me to get home every day. American children might complain that school is boring or dreary, but for these extremely poor children who never dreamed they would be students, learning was a miracle.

Word got around, and soon African parents began arriving from all over and asking me to teach their children. Some walked as far as ten miles with their barefoot children to reach me. So many people came to learn the basics of reading and math that my sister started pitching in, and then my parents got involved. Soon we had a veritable school for the poor. I saw how unfair it is when people want to learn and change their lives but have nobody to help them, and my afternoon lessons became protests against the system. I followed Bapuji's precept to be the change you want to see in the world. You can speak up with action as well as words.

Following Bapuji's example, my parents had taken a vow of poverty, so we had only the bare necessities and no savings. But compared to the black Africans around us, we were living a very comfortable life.

My mother found her own way to speak out against the inequality around us, and her actions were eloquent.

We had cows that produced more milk than we could consume, so my mother started selling the extra milk to the poor, charging them a penny a pint. She also took a penny for the excess vegetables that we grew on the farm and clothes that she collected from her friends in town. When I was old enough to realize that her prices were ridiculously low, I asked her why she charged anything at all.

"By charging a little, I am recognizing their dignity and giving them pride in the fact that they bought food or clothes for the family," she explained.

My mother was moved by compassion, not pity, and she wanted to help the people rebuild their self-confidence and self-respect so they could achieve things for themselves. Acting from compassion is much more effective than acting from pity; it also lets us build relationships between different kinds of people. My mother spoke up for the dignity of the poor, just as my grandfather did.

My grandfather had one caveat about speaking up for yourself: he didn't allow anybody, including himself, to think they were always right or above learning from another's perspective. Ashram life was designed to help people overcome prejudices and divisions and help foster understanding, acceptance, and appreciation of the differences among human beings.

Bapuji believed that to speak out credibly against injustice and hope to transform society, you had to speak from experience and feel the injustice in your bones.

Speaking out for what you believe is right can sometimes put you in a precarious position. As an adult living back in India, I began studying prejudice because I was interested in how we so foolishly set up divisions between people. One day a woman from Mississippi who was traveling through India visited my office in Mumbai, and we spoke about race in America. I thought it would be interesting to write a comparative study on discrimination in South Africa, India, and the United States. I had learned while living in South Africa that if you weren't white, you were black, and therefore different. My new friend from Mississippi told me that in America at the time, the racial divide pitted those of

African and slave descent against white Americans. In India we didn't use skin color to determine differences between people, but the caste system dictated which group you belonged to and divided people into groups like Brahmin or untouchable.

The University of Mississippi offered me a fellowship to do this cross-cultural study of prejudice, and my wife and I moved to the States. People heard that Gandhi's grandson was in America, and I was honored by how many wanted to know more about Bapuji. A year or so later, in 1988, I was invited to speak at the University of New Orleans. The school had publicized the talk, and there were posters all over inviting people to come hear "Gandhi on Racism." It happened to be the same year the racist and Ku Klux Klan member David Duke was running for the Louisiana House of Representatives.

When we landed in New Orleans, four policemen got on the plane and an announcement was made: "Mr. Gandhi, please step forward."

I stood up shakily. What had I done? The policemen wouldn't tell me what was going on, but one said, "This is for your safety." With two policemen in front of me and two behind, I was escorted off the plane and brought in a car to the university. There I was finally told that the university had received several threatening calls from the KKK, including plans to murder me.

We decided that my speech would go on. The audience was kept well away from me—the first rows of the auditorium were left empty—and I was brought out from the back of the stage at the last moment. Afterward I was whisked back to the airport and held in a special VIP room where the same four policemen stood guard. Finally, I was brought to the plane, the last to board, and settled into a first-class seat the airline had set aside for me. The policemen gave me a quick salute and left.

I learned that day that speaking out can cause upheaval, fear, and conflict long before it results in the change you want. Sometimes it's easier to keep your head down and not make noise—to eat the boiled pumpkin and figure that it's safer and less complicated to go along with the crowd. But my grandfather would never do that. Over the years he was beaten and attacked and imprisoned, and there were eight attempts on his life. On one occasion the would-be assassin was caught by volunteers, but Bapuji refused to hand him over to the police. Instead he began a conversation to find out why the man was so eager to kill him. After almost an hour Bapuji accepted that the man was unwilling to reason or change, so he let him go, saying, "Good luck to you. If I am destined to die at your hands no one can save me, and if I am not, you will not succeed."

Bapuji was willing to face his adversaries and go to jail for what he believed. He got his personal strength from his eagerness to speak out against a system he thought was wrong, and he used nonviolent methods to change it.

Some people might think my grandfather led a life of great deprivation; after all, he didn't eat much, and he lived in a mud hut and wore a poor-person's clothes. With all the admiration and renown he achieved, he could have lived in the mansion with the attendants I expected to see when I first arrived at Sevagram ashram.

Instead he found what was important and lived a life of passion and compassion. He spoke out for the universal values of goodness and love and peace, and standing up for those right and righteous positions made him happier than a feast in a palace ever could.

Some people might say that David Duke was also speaking out for what he believed when he made racist and incendiary remarks and that he had a right to speak as he did. In American law, speech is protected. But I think we fool ourselves when we pretend that all positions have equal validity. People who are full of hate and divisiveness, bullies who want to suppress everyone's ideas but their own, bring pain and despair to the world. Our goal should be to oppose such hatred.

My grandfather was shy when he was young, and in the early days of his activism he avoided making speeches. He told me his shyness turned out to be helpful because it made him careful about what he said. "A man of few words will rarely be thoughtless in his speech—he will measure every word," he told me.

—————— ❀ ❀ ❀ ——————

A man of few words will rarely be thoughtless
in his speech—he will measure every word.

I urge you to follow my grandfather's example and be thoughtful in what you say. Think about whether your words will help the world or hurt it. When you find the words that will do good, be prepared to speak them loudly.

Appreciate Solitude

Wherever he traveled, Bapuji was mobbed by people cheering and screaming for him. I didn't have a real sense of how overwhelming that could be until I joined him when he was on an overnight train to Mumbai. I was excited to be part of his small entourage and felt very special to be there. He insisted on traveling third class, but the railroad put on an extra car just for us. So even though we had no cushions and were sitting on the same hard benches as most travelers, we had the car to ourselves.

As we pulled into the first train station, I looked out the window and saw hundreds of people crowded on the platform, calling his name and reaching out to touch him. A wave of voices began chanting "Long live Gandhi," and I felt a surge of pride, basking in his reflected glory. Bapuji always stayed humble, but I hadn't quite mastered that yet. So many people admired my grandfather, and there I was, sitting next to him on the same bench! The adulation thrilled me. But when I looked over at Bapuji, I could see that he didn't care about recognition for himself. Instead he waved and spoke to people and held a cloth sack outside the train window to collect money for the poor. Everyone donated something. When one woman said, "I have no money to give," he pointed to a silver bracelet she was wearing and with a warm smile said, "That will do fine." Sure enough, she dropped the bracelet into the sack.

As we pulled away from the station, Bapuji sighed and went back to his work. But at the next station, an even larger crowd had gathered and the same scene was repeated all over again. Even though it was now the middle of the night, excited crowds appeared at the next station and the next—and at every station on our route. Passengers trying to get on or off could hardly make their way through the jostling crowds. Bapuji repeated his waving and speaking and collecting money at every stop. I quickly realized that although adulation was wonderful, it was also exhausting. There was no peace for him or anyone else on that train.

As I continued to travel with Bapuji, I discovered that whatever time of day or night he went out, adoring crowds gathered. If he traveled by car, people would line the roads for mile after mile, waving and weeping and calling his name. The routes weren't announced ahead of time, and certainly there was no social media then. In fact most of the people were living in villages with no phones, so I can't explain how they knew when he would be passing by. But some mysterious force drew them, time after time.

For political reasons Bapuji cherished the love showered on him. He knew that hundreds of thousands, even millions of people were ready to follow his suggestions and make any sacrifice he asked of them. But I soon came to understand that the adulation came at a price. Outside of the ashram, he could never find peace or solitude. Whenever he visited cities in India, throngs of people gathered in the street, chanting his name and waiting for hours to get a glimpse of him. Once Bapuji appeared and spoke or waved, the mob would disperse, only to be replaced quickly by another crowd. Bapuji liked to go to bed by 9 p.m. because he got up at 3 a.m. to meditate, and he began his full day with 5 a.m. prayers. But people stayed in the streets calling for him until late in the night, so he often got very little peaceful sleep. The relentlessness was nerve-shattering, but Bapuji never lost his cool or broke down.

A lot of people dream of being famous and imagine that celebrities like George Clooney and Angelina Jolie are secretly thrilled to be constantly besieged by fans and photographers. They think it would be great to be in the limelight and have millions of admirers. After traveling with Bapuji, I felt like a bit of a celebrity myself—and yes, it was often fun. You feel important, and it feeds your ego to be on the receiving end of love and acclaim. But I can also understand why some stars beg for privacy or retreat to private islands or gated communities or behind hedges in the Hollywood Hills. However much they thrive by being in the public eye, they also need that private time to center themselves again.

The media now makes celebrities of some people who are famous for no obvious reason. They have millions of followers on social media and post pictures of themselves strutting down a red carpet in a sequined gown or prancing on an exotic beach in a tiny bikini. Occasionally I will point to a picture on a magazine cover of someone I don't know and ask, "What has she done?," and nobody will be able to tell me. Attracting crowds and followers has always been a by-product of being an actor or politician or humanitarian. Those people have a core purpose in their lives, and the renown that comes with it is just something to cope with. But people who focus only on achieving fame have an emptiness in their lives they hope other people will fill by cheering for them and feeding their egos. Instead of achieving success because of talent, hard work, or important ideals, they are famous for being famous. Unlike real celebrities, they never seek solitude because they have no need to recharge.

Bapuji didn't have a staff of publicists and advisors to shelter him, and he certainly had no hedges to hide behind. But after keeping his public face strong, he would retreat to Sevagram for refuge. He could have located his ashram anywhere, but he chose a remote spot in central India. Given my long walk from the train station the first day I arrived, I knew how difficult it was to get there, and Bapuji wouldn't make it easier. He even asked the local government *not* to set up a bus route between Wardha (the closest town) and the ashram. He wanted people coming only if they had serious intent and weren't just trying to get a peek at the famous Gandhi.

You don't have to be a movie star or a Mahatma to need solitude—it's crucial to all of us who have a real sense of self. My grandfather often joked that he could find moments of silence in only two places: the ashram and prison. For him, preserving personal solitude was a way to fuel inner peace. Finding your own place for retreat is crucial in our busy and often overwhelming world. It doesn't have to be fancy. An hour in your own room with no distractions will suffice. So will time curled in bed, writing down thoughts in a journal. We all need to be able to take stock of our lives, to meditate and reflect, if we want to grow as individuals. After some personal time for thought and introspection, you will be able to fully connect with others in more deeply meaningful ways.

Bapuji made every Monday at the ashram a day of silence when he would catch up on his writing. On other days he didn't want just passive quiet; he believed in active reflection and meditation. He often retreated to his spinning wheel because he found the physical concentration it required allowed him to focus on his meditating. I got pretty good at spinning while I was at the ashram, and I sometimes challenged Bapuji to see which of us could go faster. He didn't mind the competition. "Arun now beats me consistently at spinning," he wrote delightedly to my parents.

Even though I sometimes turned it into a game, that time spent spinning and meditating was important to both of us. I liked being quiet and could spend hours all by myself. Grandfather lauded this trait in a letter to my parents in which he wrote, "Maintaining silence is something we all need to learn from Arun."

Many parents think they are doing a great favor to their children by keeping them busy. They fill their children's time after school with soccer games and tennis practice, with ballet classes and gymnastics training, with piano and violin lessons. The children go from one activity to another, but they never have time to just think and play and discover who they are when left to themselves. All this enrichment may be fine, but parents should also think about giving their children the gift of solitude now and then.

As adults many continue the pattern of an over-scheduled life, boasting about how much they accomplish in a day and how little sleep they get. Multitasking has become part of everyday experience, and having a fast-paced life with no time to pause, reflect, and recoup is too often the norm. This problem has existed for a long time. My grandfather had a German friend who came to visit and chided us that it was a sin to sleep away one-third of your life. Bapuji had a quick response: "Sleeping a third of your life adds a third to your life span!"

Bapuji believed that we don't need to make life faster—we need to make it more peaceful. Computers, smartphones, and digital apps have increased the pace of our lives, and it's no surprise that the advantages they bring come with downsides. We can get in touch with people thousands of miles away in a moment, but the long descriptive letters we once wrote, filled with details of our family and the environs, have mostly been replaced by short and practical e-mails. Does anyone really think that communicating in emojis will improve human relationships and add to understanding and peace?

Social media gives us friends and followers, yet our connections are often flimsier than we realize. We can't turn for comfort or help to the "friends" we know only as a Facebook photo, and it is unlikely we will convince people about an important issue like discrimination or tolerance if we make our case in a tweet. Scattered relationships don't add up to a cohesive society.

But it's also wrong to totally condemn our current technologies. If used correctly, the better communications we have can lead to positive change. A couple of years ago I sat next to my friend Deepak Chopra at a peace conference in Berlin. While he was listening to the speeches, Deepak was also busy on his smartphone, and every now and then he would announce to the crowd, "Your message has reached two million people." I was happy that my friend has two million followers on Twitter and other social media; tweeting about peace initiatives is surely better than many of the other uses of social media.

I know my grandfather would have used Twitter and Facebook and other social media, just as he used radio broadcasts to communicate his message in his day. But we can't change the world by hitting "like" on a post. Social media is useful only if it arouses people to real action. The Arab Spring is said to have been organized on social media. Repression was common all over the Middle East, and when someone started stoking the embers, sparks began to fly. People went into the streets and connected face-to-face and began to bring about the change they thought they wanted. Sadly, the same tools are used to radicalize people to do evil. The media claims that some young Arab men participate in suicide bombings because they are promised there will be bevies of maidens waiting on the other side. I don't think young Muslims really believe this ridiculous theory, but the combination of repressive regimes, stringent religious rules, and prejudice in their adoptive countries has made life so intolerable that they would rather die. My only hope is that the message of peace—whether it is spread by radio, television, or Twitter—will ultimately become more powerful than the messages of hate and hopelessness.

People have never been more connected than they are now, but sometimes it seems that they have never been more lonely. When I traveled with Bapuji, we either talked together or sat alone with our thoughts. In other words, we either related directly or we took the time to enjoy our solitude, look out the window, and just be with ourselves. Now people spend every free moment staring at their smartphones, so they are neither alone nor truly connected to others.

When Bapuji was with people, he was inspiring them, relating to them, and sharing his ideas. Then he retreated to times of solitude at the ashram, where he would regroup and confront only himself, letting his mind recharge in quiet. I have tried to learn that technique of always being fully in the place where I am. But technology can leave us in a state of in-betweenness—never really relating to others (because we are too busy glancing at our phones) and never really alone (because we are texting rather than thinking). The netherworld that technology creates leaves us feeling unharbored.

I sometimes see children sitting in restaurants or at a park while their parents are busy on their smartphones. I don't know why it is so important for the parents to be texting the office or a distant friend at that moment. But the person really getting the message is the child sitting right there, who learns that she is not worthy of her parents' full attention. I look on sadly and think how lucky I was to have had the nurturing attention of my parents and my grandfather. People around the world wanted to hear from Bapuji, but when he was with me, his focus never wandered. He made me feel heard and important. If children have your full attention when they need it, they will be better able to be independent and alone at other times.

Bapuji believed we should spend our time in pursuit of the Truth—which he always capitalized because he saw it as the goal of life. If we make an effort to understand the Truth, we will get closer to understanding what life is really about. Bapuji admitted that he had only fleeting glimpses of the Truth, but he described it as having a luster "a million times more intense than that of the sun we daily see with our eyes." We can't recognize any of that brilliance if we are constantly distracting ourselves or focusing on the trivial. The noise of conformity drowns out the silence of Truth.

Many musicians and artists say they get their creative breakthroughs in unexpected moments. A big idea occurs to them in the shower or just as they are drifting off to sleep. Some writers keep notepads by the side of their bed to jot down the words and images that come unbidden during the night. There is nothing magical about showers and beds, but often they are the only places where we are alone and allowing our minds to wander and solve problems. I learned from Bapuji that we need input from the world, seeing people and having experiences so we have a broad view, but we also need time in solitude to make sense of it.

❦❧

After we moved to America, my wife, Sunanda, and I founded the M.K. Gandhi Institute for Nonviolence and, later, the Gandhi Worldwide Education Institute. For many years I was proud to be invited to the annual Renaissance Weekend, an American invitation-only retreat for leaders in business, politics, and the arts. It's known as the "granddaddy of all ideas festivals" and is attended by former presidents, Olympians, and Nobel Prize winners. Surrounded by great minds getting together for workshops and talks on improving public policy, I felt stimulated and energized. But I knew

I needed to go back home and work hard to share the ideas with others and bring them to life. I needed the balance of outside ideas with my own quiet time to think about how I could make them real.

The constant buzz of media, activity, and ideas can make us feel energized, but we have to be careful that we're not distracting ourselves with trivia. Whatever I'm doing and however busy I may be, I try to follow Bapuji's example of recharging. So I take time every day to be with my own thoughts and meditate. A lot of people wrinkle their noses when I mention meditation and say something like, "Nope, that's not for me." Maybe meditation sounds too spiritual to them, or they imagine they would have to wear a long robe and be surrounded by incense to make it work. Let me assure you, you can wear gym clothes and sit on a park bench—all you really need to do is pause and reflect on your own life. I do that as often as I can. I turn my thoughts inward and ponder what's important for the world and what I would like to achieve for myself and others.

Now that I'm older, I know that what matters to me is living in such a way that people see me as a model for respect and love. I've started to refer to myself as a *peace farmer* because a farmer plants the seeds and expects they will germinate and produce a valuable crop. I plant the seeds of peace and nonviolence with young people and hope they will flower. I don't try to evaluate my impact by how many "likes" I get on Facebook or how often the message is retweeted. I care about having a message that speaks to who I am and recognizes that I don't live just for myself.

Grandfather once said to me, "I feel blessed for who I am, and I hope you do too." I do feel blessed every day; all of us should. Too often, no matter our age, we make the mistake of comparing ourselves to those who seem to have more than we do—more possessions, more fame, more toys. But if we open our eyes a little wider, we will notice how much sadness and deprivation also exist, and we will realize that we can use our own blessings to make a big difference.

❈ ❈ ❈

I feel blessed for who I am,
and I hope you do too.

We need those moments of quiet and solitude away from the rush of people and expectations to put our experiences in perspective. When we compare ourselves to those around us or the celebrities in the news, we can't see the bigger picture. We lose the sense of where we fit in the world. Many people find it difficult to be quiet and still these days—even I am sometimes overwhelmed by all the distractions. We can listen to music and podcasts and videos and surf the Internet. Experts say that more data has been created in the past two years than in all the centuries and millennia before then. All that rush of noise makes it even more urgent that we remember to find the small pockets of quiet for ourselves.

I speak often now at universities, which should be places where young people of different ethnicities, religions, beliefs, and cultures live and learn together. But however much the administrations try to encourage diversity with more open admissions policies, the students themselves too often undermine it. They join fraternities and sororities with people who look and think just like they do, or they demand safe zones in classrooms so they don't have to think about things that may be new or uncomfortable. I hear about schools that put "trigger warnings" on books and lectures in case some students might be shocked by an idea they don't share. How is that learning? Too many colleges have given in to this narrow-mindedness. Education needs to be more than acquiring textbook knowledge and preparing for a career to make money. My grandfather would be unhappy to see how closed off and fearful students have become at so many of America's finest universities.

Bapuji's concept of solitude didn't mean blocking yourself off from new ideas or from people who think differently than you. He wanted all ideas to flow. He listened to everyone and then used those moments when he was by himself to weigh all the positions and decide which direction he wanted to pursue. Bapuji wanted to be face-to-face with people who held different opinions; I think he would be dismayed by college students who walk out of lectures when they disagree with what is being said.

An intellectual "safe space" is really the most dangerous place to be because it keeps you from recognizing other outlooks and approaches. It is a breeding ground for prejudice and continued misunderstanding. Bapuji would surely admire schools like the University of Chicago that have made a point of saying that students should not retreat from ideas and perspectives different from their own.

Your mind should be like a room with many open windows. Let the breeze flow in from all, but refuse to be blown away by any one.

"Your mind should be like a room with many open windows," Bapuji told me. "Let the breeze flow in from all, but refuse to be blown away by any one." I think that is absolutely crucial advice. You can let the breezes of information and ideas and different viewpoints flow into your life, but they don't have to overwhelm you. Having an open mind does not mean accepting everything you hear—it just means knowing that the simple act of listening is important too.

Be part of the world and take in all the ideas you can. Then retreat to your solitude or quiet place and decide how you will use the ideas to make a better world.

Know Your Own Worth

Many people today have a cartoon image of my grandfather as a saintly man who gave up all material goods and wore as little clothing as possible. But here's a surprise: he actually understood the value of money as well as anybody. He believed that economic strength was a key to India's freedom, because he knew national independence is meaningless if you can't support yourself or your family.

On the ashram we had no economic distinctions and lived a radically simple life. We all did chores together, from working in the vegetable garden to cleaning the toilets, and we sat on the ground to eat and study and talk. When we went to meals, nobody served us, and we brought our own plates, bowls, cups, and utensils and washed them afterward. Nobody felt deprived because we all experienced the same conditions. Bapuji understood that most of us need very little to be happy. We get in trouble when we start comparing ourselves to others and think that what they have is better—and maybe worth fighting to get. Bapuji saw that ending economic disparities would be a huge step in reducing violence in the world. You can't preach nonviolence, as my grandfather did, without also recognizing the anger that gets stirred by inequality.

Bapuji tried to keep his life simple, but he also met with some of the most important people in the world. In 1930 he traveled to London to attend the first Round Table Conference organized by the British government to discuss the future of India. As always, he was wearing the handspun, hand-woven clothes, called *khadi*, that he encouraged as a way of helping the poorest rural farmers.

The *khadi* movement had taken hold and was beginning to have an effect on the British textile industry. Since many Indians were showing stirrings of independence by making their own *khadi*, the British could no longer buy all of the cotton in India at cheap prices and then sell it back as expensive, machine-made clothing.

The participants at the Round Table were invited to Buckingham Palace, and my grandfather arrived wearing his loincloth and shawl. Royal aides fretted that this wasn't proper attire to meet the king, but Bapuji just smiled and said that if King George didn't want him as he always dressed, he wouldn't attend. Reporters heard about the story and couldn't get enough of it. "Gandhi to Go to King's Party in Loin Cloth!" blared one headline. They loved the idea that he would be walking across the crimson carpets of Buckingham Palace in *khadi* and well-worn sandals. King George came in wearing the daytime formal dress of a morning coat and striped trousers, while Queen Mary stood by in a shimmering silver tea gown. When he was asked if he felt underdressed wearing a loincloth in the presence of the king, Bapuji famously quipped, "The king had enough on for both of us."

Bapuji didn't think it was wrong to want economic success—he just thought it was wrong not to lift others up with you. He didn't care about money for himself, but he was realistic and knew that his projects needed funding. So he came up with a plan. Whenever he went out, thousands of people asked for his autograph. His prayer services embraced everybody, so there were often throngs of Hindus, Muslims, Christians, Jews, and Buddhists in attendance who admired him and wanted his signature. He realized that if he charged the small fee of five rupees (less than a dime today) for every autograph, he could raise money for his social and educational programs.

The first time I went on a trip with my grandfather, I was given the job of collecting the autograph books and money and bringing them to Bapuji in a bundle to sign. I was thrilled! I felt very important to be close to Bapuji and doing something for a bigger purpose.

In those days before "selfies" and cell phone cameras, autographs of famous people were rare and special, and some were quite valuable. So after a few days of collecting, I decided I too wanted to get my grandfather's autograph. But I had no money, and I didn't know if Bapuji would make an exception for me. I told myself that because I had been helping him a lot, there was no harm in trying. I collected pieces of colored paper, cut them to the size of an average autograph book, and stapled them together. That evening after prayers, I slipped my little untidy book into the stack I took to Grandfather. Then I stood by as he began signing the books, hoping that in the rush of the moment he wouldn't notice anything amiss.

No way. Grandfather was absolutely meticulous about every dime he received. He needed money to do his work. When he came to my book and saw no money accompanying it, he paused.

"Why is there no money for this autograph?"

"Because it is my book, Bapuji, and I don't have any money."

He smiled. "So you are trying to pull the wool over my eyes? Why do you need an autograph?"

"Because everyone has one," I answered.

"Well, as you can see, everyone pays for the autograph."

"But, Bapuji, you are my grandfather!" I pleaded.

"I am glad to be your grandfather, but a rule is a rule. If everyone has to pay, you have to pay too. No exceptions for anyone."

My ego was hurt. I wanted to be special! So I blurted out, "You'll see, Bapuji, I will make you give me an autograph for free. I'll keep trying no matter how long it takes!"

"Is that so?" Bapuji's eyes twinkled and he laughed. "Let's see who wins this challenge."

The game was on. In the weeks that followed, I used every strategy I could think of to pester him into giving me an autograph. My favorite technique was to burst into the room when he was in meetings with high officials and world leaders and wave my book at him, asking him to sign. One day I ran into a meeting, loudly announcing that I needed his signature right then. Instead of getting angry, he pulled me to his chest, put his hand on my mouth, and kept the discussion going. The important politician he was speaking with looked stunned, not knowing what to make of our scene. I thought Grandfather would give in just to keep things calm, but I should have known better than to challenge a man who'd taken on the United Kingdom.

Our competition continued for several weeks. One of Bapuji's high-level guests became so irritated by my interruptions that he essentially took up my cause. "Why don't you just give him the autograph so he will leave and stop annoying us?" he asked, exasperated.

Bapuji wouldn't let him set the agenda for our relationship. "This is a challenge between me and my grandson," he replied calmly. "You need not get involved."

Bapuji never lost his temper or ordered me out of the room. He had immense control over his anger, in spite of my attempts to provoke him.

On one occasion, to pacify me, he wrote "Bapu" on a slip of paper and said, "Here is your autograph."

"That is not good enough!" I declared.

"It's all I can give," he said, with the same persistence he showed in everything.

I was starting to understand his message. After a few more days I realized that I was never going to get the autograph for free, and I finally stopped hounding him. But instead of feeling defeated, I felt proud. I knew that our little contest hadn't really been over a scrawl of ink. Instead Bapuji was giving me a lesson in value. Since he had decided that his signature was worth five rupees, it should be worth that to everyone. If he gave it away to me for free, he was lessening his own value. Equally important, our challenge showed me that even if I didn't have five rupees, I had great value. My grandfather was willing to treat me with the same respect he paid heads of state. He didn't undermine me in front of them or treat me as a distraction. My needs were as real as theirs and as worthy of attention.

❀❀❀

Though he never gave me his autograph, Bapuji offered a much greater gift. He started spending an hour every day with me, talking and listening. He had such a busy schedule I didn't know how he could manage to fit me in, but it turned out that with disciplined habits, you can accomplish a lot more than you imagine. Bapuji had me write out my own schedule—including study time, playtime, ashram chores, and prayer—and put it on the wall to show that each minute in my life too was valuable.

Bapuji helped me see that each person has special value. He exuded love and respect for everyone, young and old, rich and poor. I came to understand how important it is to appreciate our own worth as individuals. We sometimes worry that other people are better than we are, and we forget to see what it is that makes us valuable to the world. Once we feel confident in ourselves, we can recognize and honor the value of those around us, regardless of social stature or the power attributed to them by worldly standards.

Some scholars of my grandfather's life have portrayed him as being against progress and money, but that is a misreading of his values. He valued money for what it could do to end misery and help people out of desperate situations. But he didn't consider money the measure of a person's worth. He would never (ever!) think someone wearing expensive clothes and flying first class was more important than someone clothed in rags and sleeping under a bridge. I've seen photos of my grandfather in his simple *khadi* shawl meeting heads of state from around the world. The royal leaders are decked out in ornate uniforms and shiny jewels and huge hats—frankly, they're the ones who look silly to me. Bapuji didn't need an elaborate costume to let the world know of his worth.

If you use money and material gain to define your value, you may end up feeling hollow. I feel sorry for someone who tries to impress me with his premium car or oversized house, because I know that he feels something missing at his core. No amount of acquired stuff is going to fill that emptiness. On the other hand, I too often see people who think of themselves as failures because they got fired from a job or have been struggling to make a rent payment. They fear that wealthier friends look down on them, and they are embarrassed not to have more. We need to separate our self-worth from the *stuff* we have acquired.

Successful people who earn big salaries have every right to be proud of what they've accomplished, but they make a mistake if they think the size of their bank account is a reasonable measure of their worth. In fact it can be just the opposite. "Materialism and morality have an inverse relationship," Bapuji believed. "When one increases, the other decreases." He didn't mean that it was immoral to earn money or that there was something inherently honorable about being poor. He objected only to focusing on material gain to the exclusion of everything else. If money means something to you, then go ahead and work hard and make a lot of money. But always remember there is a next step beyond that.

Materialism and morality have an inverse relationship. When one increases, the other decreases.

Some of my own children and grandchildren have taken up the family cause of nonviolence and helping others. Our family now includes activists and professionals of all sorts, and I am very proud of all of them.

My grandson in India is a lawyer who works to rescue trafficked girls, and my granddaughter has been using video journalism to highlight little-known organizations doing good work in Indian villages. In America one grandson is a caring and hardworking doctor, and I am equally admiring of another grandson, who is the managing director of a well-known investment company in Los Angeles. He gets a bigger paycheck than I have ever dreamed of, but he is also showing signs of being very charitable and understanding his obligations to the bigger world. As I said, you can't use money as a measure of a person's worth in either direction.

Bapuji understood that many important things—like eradicating poverty and discrimination and giving people better health care—require infusions of money. He would never take anything for himself, but he was unabashed in asking for support for his causes. So I tried to use that model when I first came to the United States and had the idea to launch an institute for nonviolence. My wife, Sunanda, and I talked about it, and the more we imagined the workshops, seminars, and lectures we could offer, the more excited we became. We thought it would make sense to have the institute on a university campus, and I wrote to a number of university presidents, telling them about the plan. Not one of them answered. Maybe they thought the idea was too far-fetched, or they just threw the envelope unopened into the wastebasket.

Finally, a colleague connected me to the president of Christian Brothers University in Memphis, Tennessee. I went to meet him, and he enthusiastically offered us a rent-free home and office space on campus. Wonderful! I was thrilled, even though he made it very clear that the university didn't have the money to fund the institute; we'd have to do that ourselves. I accepted without knowing how my dream would play out.

I stayed awake many nights, trying to figure out how I could get the money I needed. I had images of my grandfather holding his cloth sack out the train window to collect for his good causes and charging five rupees for his autograph. His autograph! It suddenly occurred to me that I had something very valuable: a stack of his original handwritten letters, tucked away in a box in my house. The letters had been written to my parents and to us children. Copies had already been given to the Indian government, but the originals were deteriorating because I didn't have the means to properly preserve them. Should I be sentimental and just hold on to them until they completely fell apart? That seemed wrong. I knew they would be valuable to a museum or a collector, and selling them would give me money to promote the cause of nonviolence. To the question "What would Bapuji do?" the answer seemed obvious.

I got in touch with Christie's auction house, and they sent me an estimate of $110,000. Now the dream was becoming real. A dear friend (and legal advisor) helped me register the M.K. Gandhi Institute for Nonviolence as a charitable organization, a 501(c)3. I didn't want anybody to think I would be using even a cent of the proceeds for myself, so I asked Christie's to auction the letters and transfer the money directly to our brand-new institute.

The sale was announced, and that night my phone in Mississippi rang at 2 a.m. I groggily answered and was stunned to hear the office of the president of India on the other end. Apparently all hell had broken loose. Before I could say a word, the president's private secretary accused me of commercializing my grandfather's name and insisted that I stop the auction at once. I tried to explain my plan, but I may not have been very articulate at that hour. I finally hung up when I realized I wasn't having any impact.

The next day the president issued a statement to the press denouncing me for exploiting the Gandhi name. I started getting angry and abusive letters from all over India. I was shocked. Now the sleepless nights returned with a vengeance. I needed the spirit of my grandfather to give me some guidance, but I didn't hear his voice.

Late one night I thought about Bapuji's belief that all people have equal value and how, faced with a dilemma, he often asked the public what to do. So I got in touch with the *New York Times* and asked if I could send them an op-ed piece explaining my problem and asking readers to guide me. I titled it "What Should I Do?"

When the piece was published, the response was overwhelming. More than 90 percent of the people who took the time to reply said they supported my plan. Many Indian newspapers reprinted the *Times* essay, and very quickly the tide turned. Suddenly people were praising me for following the true spirit of Gandhi. People who had been attacking me viciously now lauded and blessed my effort.

All the controversy, though, scared away many would-be buyers, and when the auction took place, the letters brought in only half of what had been estimated. In a final ironic twist, I discovered that the buyer was the Indian government—which had turned down my earlier offer to sell them the letters.

❀❀❀

Bapuji believed that each of us is endowed with special talents, and it's our job to use them not just for ourselves but to build strength for others, now and in the future. There's an ad for a very expensive jewelry company that proclaims that you never actually own one of their watches; you just look after it for the next generation. I don't know much about high-priced timepieces, but I do know that the same concept applies to the deeper values we possess. Bapuji often said that however we acquired our talents—through good education, helpful family, or hard work—we don't *own* them; we are just their trustees. Our talents will be passed on by what we do and who we help, and they should be used to contribute to others as much as ourselves.

Some years ago I took a group of young women and their professors from Wellesley College on a tour of India. I wanted them to see some of the good work that was going on there and the huge difference one person can make in adding value to impoverished lives. We spent the first day visiting slum projects in Mumbai and then took an overnight train to a small town built around the sugar industry, where another project was giving hope and help. We traveled for several days and met inspiring people, but all of our accommodations were very simple. We took long bus rides over dusty roads, and most of the hotels didn't have showers—just buckets of hot and cold water that you could pour over your body to get clean. After a while the young women started grumbling that they'd really like to have a comfy bed for one night and a decent shower to wash their hair.

Finally we got to a big city that had a brand-new five-star hotel. As a promotion, we had been offered rooms at half price, which we gladly accepted. As we all stood in the ornate lobby, waiting for the rooms to be made ready, there was a burst of enthusiasm from the young students. Luxury awaited! They got their keys and went off to enjoy the amenities they'd been missing.

About thirty minutes later there was a knock on my door, and I was surprised to find several students there, looking distraught.

"Please, Mr. Gandhi, we'd like to move hotels and go someplace not so extravagant," one of them said when I opened the door.

"What's wrong? I thought you were so happy to be here."

"Our rooms are beautiful, but the windows face out to the shanties, where people are living without anything. It goes against everything we've learned this week. We shouldn't have so much when they have so little."

I appreciated their compassion but told them we would stay. The images that were causing them such distress could also be a learning experience. "Usually we live in comfort and don't have a window into the other half of the world. Tonight you can't shut it out—and we never should. Maybe the stark contrasts you're seeing will stay with you, and whenever you think of them in the future, you'll be reminded of the need to take action."

It's sometimes hard to know what to do when faced with the huge problems in the world. The students couldn't simply go over to the shanties and invite the people huddled there to spend the night in their hotel room. But recognizing the discrepancies is the first step to changing them. Or maybe the first step is *caring* about the people who are in those shanties across the street and recognizing them as individuals with worth and value. The students on that trip no longer saw the poor as an indistinguishable group that could be overlooked or ignored. Instead they recognized that each person would be as happy for a soft bed and warm shower as they were.

I admire people like Bill Gates, who don't think their wealth makes them better than anyone else. A core belief of the Bill and Melinda Gates Foundation is "All lives have equal value." They stand behind that motto every day with programs to empower the poorest people in the world. They help transform lives by offering health care and education, and they focus on ensuring that more children "survive and thrive." Bill Gates may be one of the richest people in the world, but he knows that his real worth isn't measured by the bottom line on his tax return. He proves how rich he is by caring about those who have less.

Bapuji talked often about the need to share our talents and good fortune with others, and I know he would have liked to meet Bill Gates and thank him for his good work. He also would have had great respect for the corporations that show a sense of responsibility in the world that goes beyond stock prices and shareholder returns. One example I have seen firsthand (and I know there are many others) is the Tata Group, based in Mumbai. It is one of the biggest conglomerates in India, with some thirty companies making everything from cars and steel to coffee and tea. It was started back in 1868, and the Tata family that has run it ever since maintains a commitment to what I like to call "compassionate capitalism." Instead of living like kings, the Tatas have chosen modesty for themselves; they use a significant portion of their personal and corporate profits each year to help the poorest in India get clean water, better conditions for agriculture, and a chance at an education. In the town of Jamshedpur, where Tata Steel is located, the company provides just about everything for the local workers. A few years ago one executive joked that the Tatas are so generous in providing utilities, housing, cars, and local amenities (they even run the local zoo and hospital) that "the only thing you need to bring is a wife." (Or maybe now a husband.)

The Tatas are Zoroastrians, members of an ancient religious movement that began in Persia (modern-day Iran). As happens so often with religions, the adherents faced terrible persecution when a different religion gained power, and in the seventh century many fled the country. A boat full of refugees arrived on the west coast of India, and in an audience with the king, the Zoroastrians asked him to let them stay. But the king pointed to a glass full of water on the table and said, "Just as this glass is full of water, my kingdom is full of people. We have no room to accommodate any more."

In response the leader of the refugee delegation poured a spoonful of sugar into the water and stirred it. "Just as this sugar has dissolved in the water and sweetened it, my people will dissolve into the community and sweeten it," he replied.

The king understood and allowed them to stay—and the Zoroastrian presence has sweetened the Indian community ever since.

Everyone who hears this lovely story smiles at the idea of that sweetened glass of water. But it needs to be more than a story. The king's first response is what people around the world say right now when confronted with refugees, the poor, or those of a different religion, race, or ethnicity. Why can't we instead accept that every community can use some sugar and spice?

Think of your own value in that glass of water, and make it your principle in life to be sure that you are always sweetening the glass.

Lies Are Clutter

Bapuji had high blood pressure and believed in only natural cures. While I was staying with him, he left to spend some time at a nature cure clinic run by a doctor in the town of Poona, which had pure air and a mild climate. I was thrilled that he took me with him. Even though he was there for his health, important people continued to come by to consult with him.

One morning after prayers and yoga, I sat on the steps of the clinic, enjoying the cool morning breeze and the fresh smell of flowers. I was lost in thought when someone came up behind me and put his arms around my shoulders. I spun around and was stunned to see Jawaharlal Nehru, who would soon become the first prime minster of an independent India. He was already very famous around the world and regarded as second only to my grandfather in importance in that country. It was the first time I saw him in person, and I was starstruck. I had gotten used to hanging out with Bapuji, but now to meet Nehru!

"Good morning. Would you like to join me for breakfast?" Nehru asked.

"Yes, of course," I said. I stood up, trying to stay calm, and as we walked to the dining room, he kept his arm around me.

When we settled at our table, he scanned the short menu and asked me what I wanted to eat.

"Whatever you're having," I blurted out.

"No, I'm having an omelet, and I don't think your grandfather would like you to eat that," he said. He knew Bapuji was a strict vegetarian and didn't eat eggs or fish, and he assumed that I had been raised as a vegetarian.

As it happens, he was right. But I wanted to impress him, and it suddenly seemed very important that I eat the same meal he did.

"He won't mind," I said confidently.

Nehru had too much respect for my grandfather to risk offending him, so he told me that I would need to get permission from Bapuji before I ordered.

I jumped up and ran to my grandfather's room. He was in a serious discussion with Sardar Patel, who became the deputy prime minister of independent India under Prime Minister Nehru. But at that moment breakfast seemed much more important to me than the fate of India.

"Bapuji, can I eat an omelet?" I asked excitedly.

He looked up at me with surprise: "Have you ever had eggs?" he asked.

"Yes, I ate them in South Africa," I answered. This was a blatant lie, but it tripped easily off my tongue.

"All right, then, go ahead," he said.

Lying was so easy! I ran back to Nehru and announced that grandfather didn't mind at all my having an omelet.

"I'm surprised," he said, but he ordered the omelet for me. I felt the breakfast was a great triumph. I can't say that I particularly liked the eggs, but one little lie and I was able to have what seemed to me a sophisticated breakfast with Nehru.

Some weeks later Bapuji and I were in Mumbai, and members of the Birla family, who were very wealthy Indian industrialists, invited us to stay at their opulent mansion. It was so lavish and different from the ashram that I could hardly believe we were there. I spent one afternoon exploring the gardens, which looked out on the vast expanse of the Indian Ocean. I didn't realize my parents had arrived and had gone up to the first floor to visit with Bapuji. I later learned that the first question Bapuji asked them was whether I ate eggs at home, to which they had answered, "Of course not!"

I was daydreaming in the garden when my relative Abha, who also traveled with Bapuji, tracked me down. "Bapuji wants to see you in his room. You better go right away because you're in big trouble," she said.

"What have I done?" I asked incredulously. I had been trying so hard to practice model behavior.

"Don't ask me," she said with a shrug.

I went into the mansion and was surprised to see my parents there, kneeling with their heads bowed. They didn't look up as I walked in. Everyone seemed very serious. I thought briefly how small Bapuji looked in the enormous gilded room. But his strength didn't come from his size.

My grandfather beckoned silently for me to come and sit next to him. He put his arm around my shoulders. "You remember that day in Poona when you asked me if you could eat an omelet?" he asked. "You told me you had eaten eggs before, and so I allowed it. I just asked your parents and they say they have never given you eggs to eat. So now please explain who I am to believe."

I felt my heart beating very hard. I didn't want Bapuji to lose faith in me, so I thought fast. "Bapuji, we did eat cakes and pastries at home, and I think they are made with eggs," I said earnestly.

My grandfather looked at me for a moment, taking in my point, then burst into loud laughter. "You will be a good lawyer, my son. I will accept that. Now run along and play," he said, patting me on the back.

I left the room quickly, avoiding everybody's eyes. I had been cleared, but the agony of the encounter stayed with me. All these years later I still think about it. Lying often seems like the easiest course at the moment, but when we lie to others, we are also lying to ourselves. We could gain so much more by facing the truth from the beginning. That day in Poona I pretended to Bapuji that eating an omelet was no big deal, and so I told *myself* that too. Rarely do we casually think, "I choose to be a terrible person today and lie." Instead we convince ourselves that what we're doing is—somehow!—okay. We hide the truth from ourselves as much as from others.

Avoiding lies is difficult because it requires recognizing our desires and then admitting them. How much better it would have been for both Bapuji and me if, rushing over to him that morning in Poona, I had admitted I'd never eaten eggs but that I thought it was time I did. I could have explained that I thought I was old enough to make the decision for myself whether or not to be a strict vegetarian. I might have confessed my infatuation with Nehru and discussed that too with Bapuji.

Many of us lie when we feel frustrated that we're not in control of our lives. That's a common condition among children and teenagers, who are expected to follow the rules adults set. I recently heard a very smart ten-year-old negotiating with his parents about how much longer he could stay on his computer. He had just learned coding and was excited to finish a project, but his parents insisted it was time for bed. As he ran out of real arguments ("I'm right in the middle of this!"), I could hear him veering toward some half-truths ("My teacher wants me to do this all night!"). Parents can help children avoid lies by treating their desires with honesty and respect.

It's also important that parents themselves don't slip into lying just because it's easier than telling the truth. When parents set an example of lying about little things ("The shot won't hurt"), their children learn that it's an acceptable technique.

A lot of people—children and adults—resort to lies when they feel powerless, thinking lying will make them stronger. Usually, though, lying makes you weaker. You typically get tripped up by a lie, as I did with the omelet. But even if nobody picks up on the twisted facts, your victory is only short term. By lying, you undermine your sense of self and erode the very power you were trying to achieve. You may begin to believe that you can be successful only by presenting a false face to the world.

Many people dabble in lying at some point, but hopefully they outgrow it and gain enough faith in themselves to say the truth of what they really believe. I can understand the impetus that makes children lie, but it's sad when politicians fall into the same web and offer lie after lie. Their own vanity becomes much more important than the integrity of the position they want to attain. They are trying to get elected, but they can never lead, because they are weak and insecure at the core.

Knowing the incredible person he became, it's easy to think of my grandfather as a perfect human being who resisted all temptations and never veered from absolute honesty. But none of us is perfect. Bapuji knew that lies are a very human foible. He had his own experiences being deceptive when he was young; that's probably why he let me off so easily with the egg story.

When he was about twelve years old, Bapuji fell into a trap many children find irresistible: being attracted to the forbidden. For him, that included meat and cigarettes. He watched people smoking cigarettes and thought emitting puffs of smoke from your mouth looked alluring. At first he tried to puff on the discarded stubs he found. Then he wanted to get real Indian cigarettes, and he started pilfering coins from around the house to buy them. The appeal of cigarettes soon disappeared, however. Long before anyone knew just how bad smoking is for your health, he declared it "barbarous, dirty, and harmful." He didn't like traveling in trains where people smoked; he said it made him choke.

His meat eating also involved subterfuge, but it had a slightly more noble cause. As a scrawny kid obsessed with India's freedom, Bapuji wondered how he could ever stand up to the British, who individually seemed so much bigger and braver than he was. A taunting nursery rhyme from those days claimed that the British were strong because they ate meat, and the vegetarian Hindus could never compete with them. Bapuji's closest friend was a Muslim who shared that view. "If you want to be big and strong like the British and be able to push them out of India, you need to eat meat," the boy told my grandfather.

So Bapuji decided to go on a secret diet of meat eating to bulk up. Deceiving his parents required some complicated machinations. He and his friend snuck off to a quiet spot by the river for Bapuji to try meat for the first time. He didn't like it and even had terrible nightmares afterward. But he decided to stick with it. For almost a year his Muslim friend cooked up goat and other meats for him, and Bapuji devoured his dinners on the sly. Lies led to more lies. When he came home from one of his clandestine meals and wasn't hungry for whatever his mom had made, he claimed that he had a stomachache. He even stole a piece of gold from his brother to pay for more meat.

All the sneaking around made Bapuji feel bad. And

despite all the meat he ate, he wasn't growing the way he'd hoped. It turns out eating meat doesn't make you any stronger than eating a balanced vegetarian diet! So he decided to give up meat and stop lying to his parents.

Confessing to an ongoing lie is hard, and Bapuji struggled with his conscience for a while. He couldn't bring himself to tell his parents face-to-face, so he decided to write them a letter, admitting his deception and asking forgiveness. But then he struggled with actually giving them the letter. His father was quite ill by then, and Bapuji was helping take care of him at home. One evening when the two of them were alone, he found the courage to give him the letter. His father read and reread the words, and soon both of them had tears streaming down their faces. His father finally pulled Bapuji to his chest and whispered, "I forgive you, son."

Bapuji looked back on that time with sadness. When he told me this story, he explained that a clean confession combined with a promise not to repeat the mistake can help others trust you again. But he also wanted me to know that lying and the avoidance of truth are behaviors we all struggle with. Lies are like sand; they cannot create a solid foundation. Whatever you build on top of them is shaky and insecure. If you keep piling them up, your sandcastle of lies will eventually topple.

Bapuji found out firsthand that it's better to deal with the repercussions of truth than the regret of lies. It would be nice if you could learn that lesson once and have it stick with you for life. But even Bapuji had to learn it over and over again. He lied about the cigarettes, about eating meat, and about stealing—until finally, after his confession to his father, he decided that he would never lie again. That was when he eventually wrote that Truth has "an indescribable luster, a million times more intense than that of the sun."

Bapuji made an interesting connection between lying and the complicated concept of *ahimsa*. One of the cardinal virtues in Hinduism and Buddhism and other religions, *ahimsa* holds that we should never do anything to hurt each other or ourselves. It's easy to understand how that was the basis for Bapuji's nonviolence movement, but it has a much deeper meaning that includes other kinds of harm we do. Bapuji believed that controlling our instincts to lie and deceive was a lot harder than giving up physical fighting.

Like Bapuji, I needed a couple of rounds of lying before I came out firmly on the side of telling the truth in all situations. But that is where I have ended up and will remain. When I hear how facts are distorted during political debates, I'm amazed to realize that some people would have you think truth is just whatever they want it to be. Science doesn't have all the answers, but we have to rely on the best facts we have in the search for an absolute truth. If you claim that global warming isn't real, that immigrants cause crime, or that discrimination doesn't exist, you are purposely ignoring facts and letting emotional lies win the day. Perhaps you have personal reasons to oppose immigration or support discrimination, but be honest with yourself about what those are. Don't build a future for yourself or your government on that deceptive foundation of sand. Bapuji said that his dedication to the Truth is what drew him into politics. That would be a great model for others to follow!

One man I know jokes that he gave up lying because he wasn't smart enough to remember all the stories he told and what he said to whom. He didn't want to keep cluttering up his life with lies. Whatever your reason, sticking to the truth ends up being a lot more powerful than pretending to be something you're not.

Americans praise people who are "authentic," who take on a cause or a position they truly believe in. I often think about my grandfather in his simple shawl and sandals, getting millions of people to follow him. How did he do it? I think people were drawn by the truth in his heart and the authenticity of his passion.

People speak in awe about the Salt March he led in 1930 as a nonviolent protest against British rule. Salt was a staple in the Indian diet, but locals were prohibited from collecting or selling their own salt and had to buy it from the British. A heavy tax was put on top of it too. My grandfather decided to make abolishing the salt tax a key part of his next nonviolent campaign. He had long believed that he could negotiate with the British and encourage them to be more just, so he sent a heartfelt letter to the viceroy, describing the problems and injustices he wanted corrected. The viceroy sent back a four-line reply saying only that Gandhi shouldn't break the law.

"On bended knee, I asked for bread and I received stone instead," Bapuji told his followers.

He announced then his plan to march some 240 miles to the Arabian Sea. Once there he would defy the law and collect salt from the water's edge. Just about everyone at the ashram where he was then living wanted to join him, but he picked only a few dozen to follow him. The youngest person on the march was sixteen; my grandfather, at sixty-one, was the oldest. The morning they set out, everyone at the ashram was up before dawn to see them off. A crowd of thousands from nearby towns also gathered, and reporters came from all over Europe, America, and India.

Every day of the march, my grandfather stopped in local towns along the way and explained his plan—and more and more people joined.

"This is a struggle of not one man, but millions of us," he said at one village, where some thirty thousand people had gathered to listen and pledge their support.

By the time Bapuji arrived at the sea a month later, tens of thousands were walking with him. My grandfather then famously stepped onto the beach, reached down, and took a lump of natural salt from the mud.

"With this salt, I am shaking the foundations of the empire!" he declared.

He had defied the British. Without violence or anger, he had shown that subjugating people is wrong. His friend Mahadev Desai, who was at his side, later reported that when they saw Bapuji on the beach, others in the crowd also gathered salt in their hands, laughing and singing and praying. The whole of India seemed to respond. The British soon stepped in and arrested my grandfather and some sixty thousand others. But the message had been sent, and millions more continued the civil disobedience. All along the coast, Indian nationalists gathered in huge crowds to make salt. There was not enough room in the jails for all of them.

My grandfather was not a fiery orator, and he didn't have an army or organized political party behind him. But he drew the support of tens of thousands of marchers and millions more supporters who sensed that he would speak only the deepest truths to them. He was motivated by honesty and deep belief. That is very hard to resist.

Deciding to forgo lies and follow the truth can change your life—and maybe your country.

Waste Is Violence

I enjoyed the days I spent in Poona with Bapuji. Though
I appreciated the solitude of the ashram, Poona was bigger than Sevagram, and it was nice to be able to walk
through bazaars and shops again. We stayed there long
enough that Bapuji arranged for me to have a tutor in
town, and one day as I was walking home from my lessons, I saw some nice big pencils in a store window. I
looked at the little nub of a pencil in my own hand and
decided I deserved a new one. So I tossed the nub into
the grass by the side of the road.

That evening, during my time with Grandfather, I told him that I needed a new pencil. It didn't seem like a big deal, but Bapuji never missed a thing, and he pointed out that I'd had a perfectly good one in the morning.

"It was too small," I told him.

"It didn't seem that small to me. Let me see it," he said, holding out his hand.

"Oh! I don't have it. I threw it away," I said casually.

Bapuji looked at me incredulously. "You threw it away? In that case, you will have to go find it again."

When I reminded him it was dark out, he handed me a flashlight. "This should help. I am sure if you retrace your steps and apply your mind you will find it."

Knowing there was no way out of this, I set out down the road in the dark, peering into bushes and gutters along the roadside. One person who happened to be out noticed me and asked if I was looking for something important. I felt ridiculous, but I told him the truth, that I was searching for a little pencil I had dropped. "Is it made of gold?" he asked with a laugh.

I got to the spot where I thought I had tossed the pencil nub and rummaged around in the dirt and grass. It took me two hours to find it—or at least it felt that long. When I finally grabbed it from under a bush, I didn't feel like I'd found a treasure. It was still just a tiny pencil that I didn't want. Surely when Bapuji saw it, he would understand that it hadn't been worth saving and I had been right. I rushed home jubilantly and found my grandfather.

"Here is the pencil, Bapuji. See how small it is?"

He took it and held it in his hand. "This is not small. This can be used for a couple of weeks. I'm glad you found it," he replied.

He put the pencil on his little table and smiled at me. "Now come sit beside me and I will explain why I made you look for it."

I sat down next to him and he put his arm around me. "Wasting anything is more than a bad habit. It expresses a carelessness about the world and a violence against nature."

Wasting anything is more than a bad habit. It expresses a carelessness about the world and a violence against nature.

I had previously thought of violence only in terms of hitting people, so I listened very closely.

"I want you to know that a lot of effort, money, and time are invested in making all the things that we use, even little things like this pencil. When we throw something away we are wasting the resources of the country and we are abusing the efforts of people who made things for our comfort and use."

As I considered that, Bapuji asked, "When you walk around on the streets, do you see poor people?"

"Yes, Bapuji, I do."

"Those poor people can't afford to buy a pencil, while people like us, who can buy the things we need, waste a lot of them. When we consume too many of the resources of the world, we make them even more scarce for others."

When we consume too many of the resources of the
world, we make them even more scarce for others.

"Okay, Bapuji, I understand," I mumbled.

I started to get up, but the lesson wasn't over. "I have another assignment for you. And for this you will need even more than a little pencil nub," he said, with a twinkle in his eye.

Bapuji asked me to take paper and pencil and draw a family tree of violence. He wanted me to see how so many of our actions are interrelated. This tree was to have two main branches—one for physical violence and one for passive violence. Every day he wanted me to analyze my actions and the actions of people around me and add them as branches on the tree. If I hit someone or threw a rock, I was to add a branch of physical violence. But he wanted me to be equally aware of habits and ways of life that hurt people, so every time I saw or heard about discrimination or oppression, waste or greed, I would draw a branch of passive violence.

For the next few days I worked very hard on the tree, and when I brought it to Bapuji, I proudly showed him how little physical violence there was. "I have my anger under control!" I said.

He nodded, and then we both looked at all the branches of passive violence I had noticed. "Passive violence is the fuel that ignites physical violence in the world," he explained. "If we want to put out the fire of physical violence, we have to cut the fuel supply."

Passive violence is the fuel that ignites physical violence in the world. If we want to put out the fire of physical violence, we have to cut the fuel supply.

Long before people talked about environmentalism and understood how we humans were affecting the planet, Bapuji recognized that the overconsumption of natural resources by some creates an economic imbalance for all. Materialism intelligently and compassionately used can help ensure a decent life for every person

on earth. But materialism used to exploit and abuse creates an impossible imbalance. Yet since my grandfather's
time the inequities have only gotten worse. The world's
richest 1 percent now control more than half the wealth
in the entire world. The affluent feel they have a license
to take what they want and toss the rest.

"Our greed and wasteful habits perpetuate poverty,
which is violence against humanity," Bapuji told me.

Our greed and wasteful habits perpetuate poverty,
which is violence against humanity.

Bapuji, who was opposed to wasting anything, even
a pencil nub, would hardly know what to make of our
current throwaway culture. Waste has become such a
part of our lives that we forget to think about the bigger consequences. As much as a third of the food we
buy in America ends up being thrown into the garbage,
and more is tossed away by grocery stores before it can
even be sold. We send more than $160 billion worth of

food to landfills every year. At the same time, millions of children around the world go to bed hungry every night. My grandfather used to say that so long as there are tears in the eyes of even one person in the world, humanity should not rest. The security and stability of any civilization depends on the security and stability of every individual. If we could curb overbuying and waste, we could save millions spent transporting food that will end up as garbage—and instead bring it to the places and people that really need it.

I didn't completely understand Bapuji's lesson about the pencil nub until I got a little older and opened my eyes to the imbalances in the world. You may think that making a small change in your life doesn't solve anything, but all those little actions add up. I always carry a handkerchief in my pocket, which I use instead of tissues or paper towels. Maybe it's not changing the world, but think what a difference it could make if we all did it. One report estimates that if every aluminum can in the country were recycled, we could power four million homes and save $800 million per year. That's a lot of savings from putting your beer can in a recycling bin rather than the trash!

And studies show that people feel good when they pay attention to the environment. Recycling has become so popular that most towns and cities now have recycling programs. Many of us bring reusable bags to the grocery store and carry stainless-steel water bottles instead of disposable plastic. In the global economy now, an action you take at home in suburban Indiana can have repercussions in the poorest villages in India. That's true for big issues like fighting climate change and creating better agricultural solutions to feed the world's hungry, but it's also true in a very literal way for the smallest contributions we make. Instead of sending their gently used clothing to the landfill, people are choosing donation. So it's not unusual to see barefoot Indian children wearing T-shirts with the logo of the Chicago Cubs or New England Patriots, T-shirts donated by people halfway around the world.

My grandfather believed in the power of the individual to change the world, but I understand why people wonder if their personal efforts can really mean anything in the bigger world. We read that levels of carbon dioxide in the atmosphere are rising faster than anticipated by even the most pessimistic climate-change scientist. Before too long the impact on the environment could be devastating. But what use is trying to lessen your own carbon footprint when big companies and airlines and cars are continuing to be the main cause of the trouble? Perhaps the best answer came from Bapuji's own mother, who had no education but gave my grandfather a foundation in solid wisdom. She knew the ancient Indian and Greek philosophy (which was later refined to good science) that everything is made of small, discrete parts called atoms that come together to form everything around us. She taught him that "the atom reflects the universe." From the smallest act to the largest, what we do in our own lives becomes a mirror for what the greater world will look like. Take care of your own surroundings, and the world will be a better place.

Affluence can solve many problems, but greed and insensitivity create many more. Bapuji didn't need much

more than a desk and a pencil and paper to inspire people and transform the world but most people now gather
material goods at an alarming rate. We buy and buy and
then don't know what to do with all we have. An entire
industry has arisen around helping people organize the
stuff in their homes. The books and consultants (yes,
there are organizing consultants!) usually say the first
task is to throw away most of the stuff you've collected
because you don't need it. But this begs the real question:
Why did you buy it in the first place?

Making purchases—whether shoes or sofas or diamond rings—may bring short-term gratification, but the
pleasure fades quickly. We get used to what we have, so
we turn around and buy more, hoping for a new thrill.
But no amount of stuff can fill the empty space in our
hearts. We need to learn that we will find much more joy
in things we create than in things we buy and discard.
When I was growing up in South Africa, our house was
made of corrugated iron and wood, and it was slowly
rotting away. There were gaping holes in the foundation
at ground level that my dad tried to fix, but the patches

never lasted long. We had no electricity, and in that snake-infested area, slithery creatures often found their way through the holes. I was always terrified when I got up to go to the bathroom at night.

Eventually my dad decided that we needed a new house. He brought home sand and cement so we could make the concrete blocks to use for building. We were so excited at the prospect that we all got involved in making those blocks and baking them in the sun. It took a whole year to build the house, and it felt like a huge accomplishment when we finally moved in. Sadly, that was the same month my grandmother, Bapuji's wife, died; my father named the house in her honor: Kastur Bhavan (house of). I was very proud of that house because I was part of building it.

Bapuji didn't need material goods to have an impact on the world; none of us does. The one time I tried to make myself more important by showing up with something expensive backfired on me in a humorous way. It occurred after my grandfather had died and Prime Minister Nehru invited me to join him for breakfast at his home.

Nehru and my grandfather had great respect for each other when they worked for India's independence, and Bapuji considered it a great occasion when Nehru became the country's first official prime minister. When my grandfather was assassinated, the prime minister gave a moving speech to the nation, saying, "The light has gone out of our lives and there is darkness everywhere."

I appreciated that despite the pressures of his office, Prime Minister Nehru stayed close to our family after Bapuji died, and I was happy for the breakfast invitation. His daughter, Indira Gandhi, and her husband would be there too. (Despite the coincidence of the name, he was no relation to us.)

As I didn't have a car then, I figured I would take a taxi. But my uncle, a well-to-do businessman, insisted that I must not arrive for breakfast with the prime minister in a lowly taxi. So he lent me one of his corporate limousines for the day, complete with a driver. When I arrived, Nehru wasn't at breakfast, and I asked Indira where he was. She explained that he ate fast and he didn't like to finish before everyone else and sit and wait, so he always arrived late so everyone would finish at the same time

At the breakfast we had a warm conversation about my grandfather and current politics. Nehru was working hard to mold a viable foreign policy and create some of India's great educational institutions. (We didn't know then that Indira would follow him for her own two terms as prime minister.)

Afterward Prime Minister Nehru and I stood outside talking, waiting for our cars to pick us up. His pulled up first. It was very small and unimposing, and right behind it came my huge limousine. Nehru was very familiar with my grandfather's beliefs, and he looked at me in surprise. "Aren't you embarrassed to have such a big car when mine is so much smaller?" he asked.

"I'm not embarrassed at all," I replied. "You own your car, and mine is just borrowed."

We both laughed, knowing that possessions don't define us, whether they are large or small. What mattered for the prime minister was not the size of his car but the power of his ideas. And my uncle's corporate limousine, no matter how extravagant, couldn't change who I was.

⸎

The waste of resources that Bapuji described was just the beginning of the problem. Even more shocking is how we waste and exploit living creatures for our own aggrandizement. Wealthy hunters still travel to Africa to shoot beautiful leopards and lions and elephants for sport. A Minnesota dentist sparked international outrage a few years ago when he killed a black-maned lion named Cecil who was considered a national treasure in Zimbabwe. But he didn't face any charges because the hunt had been perfectly legal. He had paid tens of thousands of dollars for the privilege of destroying a gorgeous animal. Some poor countries promote safaris as a source of revenue—but that doesn't make it right to kill these creatures. Taking advantage of a struggling country by exploiting its resources is among the most violent kinds of waste.

Perhaps saddest of all is how we toss aside individuals as carelessly as I discarded my pencil nub. One day back in 1971, my wife and I were walking through the very busy streets of Bombay, heading home after a social visit. Then as now, Bombay was an overcrowded metropolis teeming with people rushing by as beggars stood in the gutters and vendors sold their wares on the streets. Garbage that had been tossed onto the road often sat festering and attracting bugs. I was walking with my eyes down so as not to step into something unpleasant when I noticed a bundle wrapped in a colored cloth. I stepped around it, but when I saw that it was wiggling I stopped and called out to Sunanda.

In the midst of all the activity around us, we cautiously knelt down and unwrapped the cloth. Inside was an emaciated baby girl, not even three days old. We looked around to see if someone might know anything about her, but nobody paid any attention to us. My wife guarded the child while I went to the nearest store to call the police. They took a while to come because this wasn't an emergency to them, and they later told us they found abandoned babies often. They took the little bundle from my wife and said they would bring the child to the Government Remand Home, a state-run orphanage. I was working then as a reporter for the *Times of India*, a leading daily newspaper, and I asked if I could come along. They shrugged and said sure.

I suppose if you see anguish all the time, you stop noticing, but I was stunned to get to the home and see dozens and dozens of babies and children who had been lost, abandoned, or orphaned. The police told me they made some attempts to find the children's parents or relatives, but the numbers were overwhelming and the success rate was less than 5 percent. The children languished and sometimes died. I wondered what would happen to the baby girl we had found. The matron of the home explained that malnourished baby girls seemed to have more resilience than the boys and a better chance of surviving.

Still, the children at the home didn't have much hope. Staff were poorly paid and often stole money or took some of the food meant for the children. Because it was run by the government, this home at least had some oversight. In small towns and villages, the mortality rate at the orphanages approached 80 percent. If the children did survive, they were sent into the world at age eighteen, often without a soul they could turn to for help or protection. Many of the girls were lured into prostitution, and many of the boys ended up in gangs, where they learned to commit petty theft and slowly graduated to bigger crimes.

I had learned from Bapuji that waste is violence—and the waste of young lives seemed exactly the kind of passive violence he had tried to teach me about during the pencil escapade. I knew I needed to do something. I visited many orphanages and shelters. At one I was surprised to see a couple with blond hair and blue eyes holding a little Indian baby. Talking to them I discovered they were from Sweden and had started a complicated legal process to adopt the baby they were holding. They introduced me to a Swedish man named Leif who had already adopted an Indian baby and had come to help them with the process. They needed some protection because unscrupulous middlemen often intervened to make money off the babies.

Leif and I stayed in touch, and he convinced me that many other Swedish families would want to adopt babies, but they needed someone honest to help them through the process. Would I think about getting involved? I knew Bapuji would want me to say yes.

Over the next dozen years my wife and I found homes for 128 babies—placing some in Sweden, some in India, and one in France. Our experiences ranged from exhilarating to heartbreaking. We would get a baby assigned to a family, then place it in a private nursing home for the three months it took to complete the legal documentation. Our hope was that the baby would gain weight and become healthy. Usually we were lucky—but at least a dozen of the babies died. I wouldn't abandon them; often I personally carried their tiny bodies to the cemetery and performed their last rites. Once I walked several miles through the streets to get to the nearest cemetery, thinking all the time of Bapuji saying that we must end the inequality in the world.

The families who got babies were often thrilled beyond measure. We met one Indian woman who had been told she was infertile and couldn't have a child on her own. We found her a baby girl and she was ecstatic. She and her husband treated us as though we were divine spirits for bringing such joy to their marriage. Several months later we heard that she had unexpectedly become pregnant, and tests showed she would deliver a healthy baby boy.

Sunanda and I were happy for her, but we were also worried. Boys are held in high esteem in Indian households, and now the baby girl would face a double disadvantage, being both adopted and female. We fretted that she would be relegated to a secondary position or maybe even treated badly. So we decided to have a frank talk with the parents and suggest that we take back the baby girl.

"She is our princess," cried the mother. "She brought us good luck and we love her. We will do anything to keep her." She and her husband both started to weep, and we realized they were genuinely mortified. We had to remind ourselves that for all the waste and violence in the world, there is still much good. We stayed in touch with the parents and enjoyed watching both children growing up happily together.

Most of the adoptive parents kept in touch with us and sent us photographs of the babies. An exception was a couple in Paris, who cut all ties with us as soon as they had their baby girl. They never responded to our letters, and after a while we gave up and just sent prayers that all was well.

More than two decades later, I got a message through the M.K. Gandhi Institute for Nonviolence that a woman in France was trying to reach me. I had no idea who she was nor why she wanted to talk with me. She called again and left another message, begging me to call her, and so I did. The young woman, whose name was Sophie, told me that she had been adopted as a baby, but her parents would never discuss her background. Whenever she asked, they said, "That part of your life is unimportant, so just forget about it." Now twenty-six years old, Sophie had recently rummaged through her father's old papers and found a document with my name on it and dated the year she was born. She concluded that I might be her biological father, or at least would know something about her past. So she Googled me and tracked me down.

I realized that she was the baby we had given to the French couple all those years ago. We spoke for more than an hour, and she sobbed while I tried to give her whatever details I could about her past. She asked a lot of questions that I couldn't answer because I didn't have any paperwork to remind me of her case. In India, Sunanda and I had lived in a 350-square-foot apartment and didn't have the luxury of hanging on to records. The consultants who help people organize their stuff wouldn't have had much to do with us: we threw everything away after a few months.

Sophie called three more times during the week. Hearing my voice was nice, she said, but she really wanted to meet me. She would plan a trip to Rochester, New York, where I was then living. Two days later she called back crying; she had discovered how expensive the airline ticket was and she couldn't afford it. But life takes happy twists too, and I had some good news. I had just been invited to speak at the Edinburgh Festival and would be in Scotland for a week. Getting there from Paris was surely less expensive.

And so in Edinburgh I spent a week getting to know this lovely young woman. She called me her "spiritual father," and now we keep in touch regularly. I am glad to have her as one of my children.

I'd had a similar experience some years earlier when we had a reunion of the Indian babies who had gone to Sweden and were now in their teens. Many of them said they wanted my help in finding their biological parents. "Ever since we started going to school, we heard all the children speak about whose eyes they have and whose hair," one explained to me. "We don't know anything about our parents. We don't know what we inherited from our mother and what from our father." I had not thought much about that before; most of us take those details for granted, but they become important when you have been denied a connection to your past.

However, as with Sophie, I had to tell them that the records of their birth were gone—if there had ever been any—and there would be no easy way to find their biological parents.

"Then there is this reality," I said. "Your biological mother took the painful decision of abandoning you in the hope that you would be able to have better lives. Maybe she was able to continue her education and is now doing well. That is what she would want for you too. We rescued you with good intentions. In the orphanage you might have died before you ever got to this age. Now you have loving parents and some happiness and security. If you think we made a mistake and ruined your life, then please forgive us."

The children gathered around and hugged me and Sunanda, all of us weeping. One teenager asked permission to think of us as her grandparents, and we said yes. That led to another girl's saying delightedly, "You've solved our problem! Now we can tell everyone we look like our grandparents."

Some years later we had another reunion in Sweden; the children were now grown up, most of them married and with children of their own. As I looked at them I thought how precious each individual can be if we take the time to nurture and care for them. Because every action multiplies, the small steps my wife and I had taken mattered on a grander scale than we realized at the time.

The passive violence of waste can be just as destructive as physical violence. Sometimes it is tempting to think, "I am just one of seven billion people. What difference can I make?" We are all connected in a great network. At a time when violence is rampant—on our streets, in our thinking and our speech, and in global politics—and peace seems ever elusive, we must recognize that nonviolence involves much more than restraint of power and reckless anger. It is deeply nuanced and rooted in how we view the world and approach each act. Bapuji sent me back to find that pencil nub as a lesson that we need "to be the change we wish to see in the world." If you don't like waste and how it contributes to inequity, if you are stunned that CEOs in America now earn two hundred times as much as the average worker, you have to start by taking a personal stand.

Bapuji disliked waste of any kind, but he could also have a sense of humor about the few things he did consider worthless and not worth saving. While I lived with him on the ashram, one of my jobs was to help open the sacks full of mail that he received every day. It was an important assignment. Long before recycling was in vogue, he practiced it every day. I was taught to pry apart each envelope carefully so that he could write his reply on the blank side and save paper.

Bapuji was in the midst of all the controversy that surrounded the potential independence of India from Great Britain. When he was at the Round Table Conference in 1931 discussing the future of India, a British official gave him a fat envelope. That night Bapuji read the letter inside, which was full of vitriol and misstatements. He removed the pin holding the pages together and saw that no page had enough blank space for a reply, so he threw them all away.

The next morning the official asked Grandfather if he had read the letter and what his response was.

"I saved the two most precious things in the letter,"

Bapuji replied, "the envelope and the pin holding the pages. The rest was garbage."

We laughed at the story, but it held a deeper truth. Bapuji worried that we waste our minds on things that don't matter and forget to study what's really important. He had no time for rancor and acrimony.

I sometimes think how much more Bapuji could have done had he lived a little longer. He felt deeply the need to fill his every moment with something that mattered, but he had the wisdom to know that we can't predict how much time we will have. The ultimate and most violent waste is to squander any part of our day. At the ashram he had me keep a precise schedule, and my days from the time I woke up until the moment I went to sleep were carefully planned out. Now, as I get older, I understand even more completely what he meant when he told me, "Time is too precious to waste."

Practice Nonviolent Parenting

Whenever I think about my time with Bapuji at the ashram, I remember his warmth and wisdom and gentle smile. He taught with love and patience.

A couple who lived near the ashram came to Bapuji one day with their six-year-old son, Anil. The little boy's doctor had said he needed to drastically cut down on his sweets because the sugar was making him ill. Anil liked his candy and would sneak treats, making himself sicker. After a few weeks of struggling, the mother brought Anil to Bapuji with a request to speak to the child about not eating sweets. Bapuji said, "Come back in two weeks."

The mother was a little frustrated and not sure why they had to wait, but when they came back, Bapuji pulled Anil close and whispered to him. They gave each other a high five—and the mother was astonished in the following days to see Anil avoiding sweets and eating as he should. He became healthier, and the mom was convinced that Bapuji had performed a miracle. She came back and asked what he had done.

"It was no miracle," he said with a smile. "I needed to give up eating sweets myself before I would ask him to do the same. When you came back, I said that I had given up eating sweets for two weeks, and now would he try?"

Bapuji's idea of education was different from most people's. He thought children didn't learn as much from textbooks as from the character and example of the people teaching them. He would scoff at the old advice "Do what I say, not what I do"; he firmly believed that teachers needed to do exactly what they asked of their students. He urged parents and teachers to "live what we want our children to learn."

I had a tutor for subjects like math and science, but Bapuji knew the most profound lessons would come from watching him. He was a kind and patient teacher, and he wanted everybody to think of him as the father or grandfather they could learn from. He first took on that role back in 1910 when he lived on the Tolstoy Farm in South Africa, one of his early experiments in having many people live and work together. He described it as a family where he had the role of father and the responsibility for teaching the children. In those days he didn't think he could find any teachers or tutors to come for the nonwhite children, so he himself began educating the boys and girls living there.

Bapuji's model of leading by example is a powerful one that parents today could use. Many parents talk about limiting screen time for their children, but then they themselves take phone calls or stare at their smartphones when they are supposed to be spending time with their families. The children learn that the phone or electronic device is more important than anything else—and certainly more important than they. I shake my head when I see parents devouring sweet pastries and frosted cereals while insisting that their toddlers eat fruits and vegetables. They are forgetting that children learn from how we adults live.

Before I went to Bapuji's ashram, I didn't have much use for school because my teachers set a terrible example. Given the racial prejudice in South Africa, there weren't many schools that would accept nonwhite children. When I was about six years old, my parents found a Catholic convent school we could attend, but it was eighteen miles away, in the city of Durban. I went there with my sister Sita, who was six years older than I. Every morning, we woke up at 5 a.m. and quickly got ready for our long, arduous trip. First we walked a mile through sugarcane plantations to the bus stop, then took a bus to the railroad station four miles away, and finally got a train into town. After that we had a two-mile walk from the station to the school. At the end of the day we had to do the whole thing in reverse.

The principal of the convent school, Sister Regis, was coldhearted and authoritarian. Lessons started at 8:20, and if you weren't inside the compound by then, you had to go to her office, where she whacked you with her polished cane. My sister and I were marched into that office and whacked more times than I want to remember. Sister Regis knew that Sita and I had to rely on the bus and train to get to school, and we couldn't do anything if either was late; we were well-behaved children who didn't oversleep, and her beating us served no purpose. But she did it anyway.

All of that violent whacking did nothing to improve my attitude—and it certainly couldn't help me be on time more often. All it did was turn me into an angry child who loathed going to school. Psychologists now tell us that children who are hit are more likely to be violent later in life, and my own experience tells me that's very true. When I left Sister Regis's office with my skin stinging from her cane, I felt powerless and angry, and all I wanted to do was hit someone. An adult beating a child only sets up a useless cycle of violence.

Years later, conducting a workshop for teachers in Memphis I was shocked when one teacher after another insisted that the best way to discipline children was to paddle or spank them. One teacher explained that after she hit the children in her classroom enough, they learned to fear her, so all she had to do was glare at them to get them to behave. She might have been proud of her approach, but, as with Sister Regis, the long-lasting results could only be damaging. Not only was this teacher educating her children in violence, but she had to continually escalate her own violence to keep control. Her method of teaching breeds disrespect. Her students had been dehumanized.

I was stunned that this kind of violent teaching would be accepted in American schools, but I am even more shocked to discover that today nineteen states still allow physical punishment. Estimates find that some 200,000 children are beaten in our schools every year by adults in authority. We need to stop calling this "discipline" and admit that it is violence against our children. We are allowing those in power (the teachers and principals) to get out their frustrations by attacking power-less children. Parents and teachers resort to hitting only when they are too weak in themselves to handle better and more sophisticated forms of teaching.

However, some parents who now shun physical violence resort to equally damaging techniques. I cringed when I heard a story recently of a teenager made to stand outside wearing a sign saying "I'm a bully. Honk if you hate bullies." It seems to me that the parent who demanded that punishment was the real bully. What is bullying if not using your power to humiliate someone you perceive to be weaker than yourself? The repercussions of shaming children this way—using emotional violence against them—can be severe. I was shocked when I heard about a father who hacked off his thirteen-year-old daughter's long hair to punish her for sending racy photos to a boy at school. He videotaped her trembling afterward as he taunted, "Was it worth it?" The video ended up on YouTube. Shortly afterward the young girl jumped off a bridge and killed herself.

While many factors often contribute to a teenager's suicide, surely the grieving father now asks the same question about his own violence: Was it worth it?

Bapuji believed in teaching children using only nonviolent means, which is much subtler than just avoiding physical confrontation. To raise your children in a spirit of nonviolence means filling your home with love and respect and a common purpose. When parents and teenagers disagree on rules, parents sometimes resort to demanding, "This is my house, and you'll obey my rules as long as you live here." That sends a message of conflict and hostility, with parents and children taking sides against each other. In a nonviolent approach, parents and children look for common ground and reasons to help and support each other. The parents accept that the children's failings are probably a result of the parents' own failings.

I experienced the power of nonviolent parenting when I was about sixteen and my dad asked me to drive him into town in the family car and do some chores while he attended a conference. Living in a rural community in South Africa, I didn't get to go into town very often, and I was excited for the chance to explore. I had heard a lot about American movies, and though I didn't think my parents would approve, I hoped to get all the chores done and sneak in a movie too.

When I dropped off my father at his conference in the morning, he asked me to pick him up at the same place at 5 p.m. Mom needed me to get groceries and do a few other errands, and my father's list for the day included getting the car serviced and the oil changed. "You have the whole day, so it shouldn't be a problem," he said.

I got the errands finished in record time and then dropped the car at the garage in time to make a 2 p.m. movie. I hunkered down in my seat, delighted by my good planning, and became riveted by the John Wayne movie on the screen, which was as good as I'd hoped. When it finished at about 3:30, I realized it was a double feature, so another movie was about to start. I quickly calculated that I could watch the first half hour or so and still be on time for my father. But (as might have been expected) I became so engrossed in the movie that

I stayed in my seat until it ended at 5:30. Oh no! I raced to the garage and got the car, but I didn't pull up at the conference center until after 6 p.m.

My dad was relieved to see me; he had obviously been worried. "Why are you so late?" he asked as he got into the car.

I was too embarrassed to tell him how much fun I'd had watching violent Westerns. You might think that after my experiences at the ashram and with Nehru, I would have known not to lie. But protecting our own image of ourselves sometimes outweighs any common sense. "The car wasn't ready," I answered, thinking up a quick excuse. But even as I said the words, I could see the disappointment on my father's face.

"That's not what the garage told me when I called them," he said. He seemed to think for a moment before deciding what to do, and then he gently shook his head. "I'm sorry you lied to me today. I have failed as a parent to give you the confidence and courage to tell the truth. As penance for my shortcomings, I am going to walk home."

He opened the car door, got out, and started down the road on foot. I jumped out of the car and ran after him to apologize. But he kept walking. I tried to talk him out of his plan and promised that I would never lie to him again, but he just shook his head. "Somewhere I made a mistake. I will take this walk to think how I could have better taught you to know the importance of telling the truth."

Mortified, I ran back to the car. I couldn't keep walking with my father because I had to get the car back home. But there was no way I would drive off and leave him to walk by himself on the dark country roads. So I drove behind him, crawling along at walking speed for the next six hours, my headlights lighting the way. The walk might have been hard for him, but it was torture for me. My father was suffering for my dishonesty. Instead of punishing me, he took the burden on himself.

My mother was expecting us home for dinner, and I knew she would be terribly worried. In those days there were no cell phones, and even if we could find a public phone, it was difficult to place a call outside the city. I imagined my mother standing on the terrace with my sisters, peering into the dark to see if she could spot our car. It was close to midnight when she finally saw the headlights creeping ever so slowly toward the house. She assumed that we were delayed by some mechanical problem with the car. It was only when we went inside that she learned what had happened.

Had my father simply punished me, I am sure I would have felt humiliated instead of guilty, and the humiliation would have led to disobedience and revenge—or a desire to hurt someone else. By using the nonviolent method he had learned from Bapuji, my father made me his partner in both the problem and the need to correct it. The impact of that is powerful and long-lasting and will achieve more positive results than coercive or violent approaches. Bapuji's method helps parents achieve their goal of raising confident, emotionally intelligent, engaged children.

Children flourish when they are respected and see that the adults in their lives aren't asking them to do something they would never undertake themselves.

The goal is to make our children good and strong people who are not victims of other kids' bad behavior. The news is full of images of kids attacking each other while friends stand by recording the action with their phones. Bapuji would not ask "What's happening to our children?" because the answer would be clear to him: we can't blame children for being callous or uncaring if we haven't shown them what positive values look like.

Parents buy their children fashionable clothes and the latest toys, but the children still want more. So the parents complain that they aren't grateful. Many children in America live in their own bubble of privilege and never see any other way of life. How can they appreciate all they have when they have no way to compare? Gratitude comes when you can see your place in the bigger world. We all do better when we have a sense of connection with each other.

When my two children were young, they wanted to have birthday parties, as all kids do. My wife and I love our children very much and wanted to celebrate their big days, but after the experiences we'd had working to get

Indian orphans adopted by loving families, we wanted our children to understand what it meant to have a family and people who care about you. We decided we would have their birthday parties in a local orphanage so that all the children could celebrate and have fun together.

"Why would we have a party with strangers?" my daughter asked me. "Why can't we invite our regular friends?"

"Sharing with people who already have a lot doesn't make much sense," I explained. "We want to give to those who have less."

She and her brother were not convinced this was a good plan until we visited one of the orphanages. This one wasn't much different from the ones that had inspired us to take action; it was bleak and dark and paint was peeling everywhere. The children had no toys. Some of the little ones were just sitting on the ground, rocking back and forth to comfort themselves. They had nothing to hold or touch or play with. My children were shocked. After that they started taking toys to the orphanage. One time we brought tricycles; the orphans had never seen anything like them before and didn't even know to sit on them or push the pedals.

Once my children talked to the orphans and spent time with them, they had a new view of their own birthday parties. Sharing with those who had so much less than they did seemed to make sense. These strangers were no longer so strange.

Given the right example, children grasp the power of nonviolence immediately. After learning that the teachers in Memphis believed in physical punishment, I thought I could begin to change attitudes by running a conflict resolution course. It was clear to me that the children needed a nonviolent model for solving problems, which they weren't getting from the adults in their lives. The first course I conducted was in a middle school. The children were excited at the chance to learn how to become peer mediators. I explained that their job was to bring two people who were disagreeing to a neutral place where they could sit across from each other with the mediator in the middle. The mediator had to lead the conversation with certain rules—making sure that each person spoke without anger and listened carefully before replying.

The children practiced with each other, and while they felt awkward at first, they soon saw how effective this simple technique could be. They learned that disagreements can be settled respectfully and without violence. They got a sense of control over their own lives, knowing they could handle conflict without resorting to fights and shouts and anger. I heard afterward that one of the young boys went home that evening and heard his parents screaming at each other. At first he cowered in his room, as he usually did in that situation, but then he got up his courage and marched out.

"I am now a certified peer mediator and I can help solve this conflict," he announced boldly. "I want you two to sit across from each other and I will mediate."

The parents were so shocked by the boy's quiet wisdom that they immediately calmed down and apologized to him. There were hugs all around.

Many of us write a will to distribute our material legacy—the money or house or diamond ring we want to pass along to the next generation. But what about the ethical legacy we leave? Our parenting style—and whether we give or withhold our love—resounds for generations. Bapuji's first exposure to nonviolent parenting and the power of love came from his own parents. When he did something wrong (and he wasn't perfect, as we've already seen), his parents responded with love and understanding. I described earlier how Bapuji wrote a letter to his parents admitting to a lie, and his father cried and embraced him. Bapuji later wrote that his father "helped me wash my sins away in tears." If his father had slapped him or shamed him or confined him to his room, would my grandfather have become a different person? An angry or vengeful Gandhi could not have influenced the world as he did. Perhaps it's not too much to say that the fate of millions might rest on the love or anger we show our own children.

It seems clear to me that if love, respect, and compassion can make a difference in one home, they can have an effect in many homes. And if in many homes, why not throughout the country and the world? The first seed of nonviolent living was planted in my grandfather during childhood, and he nurtured it throughout his life. Some people now revere him as a saint, but he didn't see himself that way at all. He tried hard to project himself as an ordinary person with ordinary failings who transformed himself in the same way that everybody can: by hard work and caring. When I was with him at the ashram, he made me promise that I would strive every day to be better than I was the day before. Once you have that goal in mind, it sticks with you. I think about it every morning when I wake up.

When Bapuji went through the normal challenges of being a teenager, he strayed from good values. Yes, that happens to even the most noble among us! But instead of going deeper and deeper into the hole of deception, he was changed by the love of his family. Many parents now are good at saying "I love you" to their children, but Bapuji's parents expressed their unconditional love without using those words. To them, their children came first in all of life's equations and were never a burden or a sacrifice. He benefited by feeling their love in everyday interactions. Instead of complaining that you can no longer go to parties or enjoy the pleasures of a single life, give your children one of the greatest gifts you have to offer: let them know that now *they* are your truest pleasure.

I worry that in our daily life, we too often set a model where "happy and kind" is less important than "rich and successful." Even though, as new parents, almost all of us say that what we most want for our children is for them to be happy, we start putting pressure on them—and on ourselves—as they get older. Progressing in our careers or making lots of money becomes more important than time spent at home nurturing love and trust and understanding. Expensive gifts replace love and attention. I don't pretend that balancing work and family is easy for anyone, and I admire the men and women who do everything they can to have full lives. But we have to be careful that we aren't worrying about the wrong values and putting emphasis on ephemeral experiences rather than long-lasting benefits and worth.

When we moved to America and lived on a university campus, my wife and I often invited students to bring their lunch and join us to talk about nonviolence and love and Bapuji's philosophy. My wife is a very kind and motherly sort, and she would hug the students and ask them how they were doing and if there was anything they needed or wanted to discuss. I remember one student who returned her embrace and began to cry in her arms. "My own parents never ask me questions like that," she said. "I wish they cared about me in the way you do."

Her parents probably loved her, but they might have been too self-absorbed and distracted by their own needs to find out what moved and inspired her.

When my daughter was raising her own children in New York State, she followed the tradition that my wife and I had set in India of serving family dinner every night at 7 p.m. Whatever else they were doing, the children knew to be home to gather at the table. It worked just fine when her children were young, but when they reached high school, some of their friends wondered why they had to run home each evening. My daughter suggested they invite their friends to join them and experience the family tradition.

One friend who came over sat at the table wide-eyed as the family shared stories and talked about what had happened during the day. She finally admitted that it was the first time she'd had a family dinner. Both of her parents worked, and everybody was expected to cook and eat on their own. "We just raid the refrigerator when we get home and nobody really cares what we do," she said with tears in her eyes. Experiencing the love in my daughter's family, she wanted it for herself.

Children want to prove their independence, so they act as if being around parents is a burden rather than a pleasure. But at heart they are deeply in need of love and understanding. When parents are too busy to provide love, they are doing a violent disservice to their children's sense of wholeness and hope.

※

My grandfather's extraordinary mental discipline left many people in awe. He had his first experience with the power of mental resolve when he was barely five years old. His mother followed the Hindu tradition of taking vows—which usually meant giving up something for a period of time—and when my grandfather was just a toddler, she vowed not to eat until she saw the sun. Under normal conditions that wouldn't be a big deal, but she took the vow during the monsoon season. Bapuji recalled later that the sun was shrouded by dark clouds for several consecutive days, and while his mother continued to cook cheerfully for the family and join them at meals, she wouldn't eat a morsel of food. Bapuji got agitated seeing her endure such a sacrifice for so long. It was perhaps his first experience of empathy.

One afternoon he sat by the window praying that the clouds would part and let the sun peep through. Suddenly a ray of sun appeared, and he called excitedly for his mother to come. But by the time she left what she was doing and got to the window, the sun had disappeared again behind the rain clouds. She simply smiled and said, "It seems God does not want me to eat today."

A vow such as Bapuji's mother took might seem strange now, in our self-indulgent society. But it had a profound impact on my grandfather. Later in his life he undertook lengthy fasts for political causes that got the attention of people around the world. These fasts were possible only because he had practiced his mental resolve early. When I was at the ashram, he observed every Monday as a day of silence, and he often undertook short fasts to gain discipline and control over his mind and desires. All of these choices emerged from the model of his mother when he was just a toddler. He used the emotional power she showed him to influence others in later years.

We don't always realize how deeply our attitudes affect our children. They sense our love as well as our distraction and take in the lessons we teach by our daily actions. If you are a parent, what example are you setting that will reappear in your children's lives and experiences later? Or if you *have* a parent (and yes, we all do!) what lessons did your parents pass on to you that you want to shake free of now? Sometimes we unwittingly repeat the violence and shaming that we experienced as children, extending a damaging legacy that should end. We can make a conscious effort to bring nonviolent parenting into our lives and give that gift to our children—and the world beyond.

Bapuji and his wife had four sons, including my father, Manilal, who was the second oldest. My father and his younger brothers, Davadas and Ramdas, tried hard to emulate Bapuji and follow his instincts for goodness and giving. But the oldest son, Harilal, was defiant from an early age and never outgrew his problems. As an adult he was an alcoholic who was accused of theft and embezzlement. My grandfather blamed himself for his son's failures and wanted to help him. But doing penance for a child's actions (as my father did when I lied about the car) works only if the child is willing to hear and reform. Harilal had no such intention. Bapuji tried to welcome Harilal home, but the prodigal son had no interest in returning to the family fold. He spent some years destitute and homeless, and he was scornful of anything my grandfather did. He seemed to devote his life to seeing how he could undermine the Gandhi name.

At one point Harilal went to a mosque in Delhi and made a great show of converting from Hinduism to Islam. My grandfather was accepting of all religions, so having a son become a Muslim wouldn't have pained him at all. But it turned out that Harilal didn't care about any religion and had just done it for the money. In the religious tensions of the time, some people thought they could embarrass Bapuji through his son: Harilal had essentially sold himself to the highest bidder. "I must confess that this has hurt me," Bapuji wrote in a letter. He believed religion should come from a pure heart and was distraught that his son would debase the search for goodness and truth out of childish rebelliousness.

Harilal had been raised with the same kindness and love and moral guidance that my grandparents gave to my father and his brothers. So no matter how many times I review this story, I can't see how Bapuji was to blame for Harilal's failures. When parents have done everything they can and problems persist, they have to forgive themselves. Nature sometimes creates a negative temperament no matter how ardently and honorably we nurture our children.

❀❀❀

Having a practical skill may be important, but so is having a profound understanding of the world. When Bapuji taught children like me at the ashram, his goal was to impart wisdom, not just facts. He believed the best education helped you deal with relationships and emotions and taught you to build a cooperative society rather than a competitive society. In the many years since he passed along his wisdom to me, some psychologists and educators have come around to his way of thinking and now talk about the need for "emotional intelligence."

Bapuji once told me a story from Indian scripture about a king who sent his only son into the world to get an education. The boy came back sure that he knew everything and was wiser than others. But the king wasn't so sure. "Have you learned how to know that which is unknown and how to fathom the unfathomable?" the king asked.

"No, that's not possible," replied the son.

The king asked him to go to the kitchen and get a fig, and when he brought it back, the king had him cut it in half. They both looked at the many tiny fig seeds. "Cut one of the seeds in half and tell me what you find," said the king.

The boy tried to cut it, but it was so small that it slipped away. "There's nothing here," he said.

The king nodded. "From what you consider nothing, a huge tree emerges. That 'nothing' is the seed of life. When you learn what such nothingness is, your education will be complete."

❦❧

Bapuji had endless patience and would take all the time necessary to teach me and the world the lessons we needed to learn. He remained calm in the face of upheavals and distractions. He wanted to understand the bigger mysteries of the world, and he knew that even the tiniest fig seed planted in the right soil could lead to something great.

We must not waste the chance to understand the world and to look for greater truths beyond what we can see and understand.

· LESSON EIGHT ·

Humility Is Strength

Many people came to visit my grandfather at Seva-gram ashram. One day a young man arrived who had just returned from England with a doctorate degree from the London School of Economics. He was smart and quick and raring to transform the Indian economy. His father was a prominent industrialist, and both parents were friends of my grandfather and held him in high esteem. They suggested that before their son, Shriman, took any action, he should get Gandhi's blessing.

So Shriman came to Sevagram. For almost half an hour he boasted to Bapuji about his achievements and explained how he was going to change the economy of the country. Bapuji listened patiently.

"Now please give me your blessing so I can get to work," Shriman said.

"You will have to earn my blessing," Bapuji responded.

"What do you want me to do?"

"Join us and clean the ashram toilets."

Shriman was aghast. "I have a PhD from the London School of Economics, and you want me to waste my time cleaning toilets?"

"Yes, if you want my blessing," Bapuji calmly said.

Shriman left the room in disbelief. He spent the night and the next morning at the ashram and reluctantly participated in cleaning the toilet buckets with the rest of us. He then scrubbed himself as clean as he could and went back to Bapuji. "I have done what you asked. Now give me your blessing."

"Not so fast," my grandfather said with a smile. "You will get my blessing when I am convinced that you clean toilets as enthusiastically as you want to go out and change the economy of the country."

Bapuji wasn't being difficult; he recognized Shriman's inflated sense of his own importance and knew that it would get in the way of his making any real changes. If you have a big ego, you have a harder time showing respect and compassion to other people, and you more easily accept caste and class distinctions. Sure that you are right, you can't see another person's point of view. My grandfather wanted to help the poor, and he felt that to truly understand their needs, he needed to live as they did. So life at the ashram was as simple as it would be for the poorest in the country. Similarly, across India, members of the lowest caste, called "untouchables," performed all the lowly labors, such as cleaning latrines and hauling waste. Bapuji sensed that if Shriman wanted to transform the economy in a way that would help everyone, he needed to understand their lives.

Even when he was in the midst of world-changing negotiations about the future of India, Bapuji remained humble. He didn't consider humility a sign of weakness or meekness—quite the opposite. He saw the damage and divisiveness that arrogance could cause. Believing that you are better than someone else leads to anger and violence and makes you blind to how closely connected we all are. When you lack humility, you scorn people who are struggling; you snub refugees because you can't see that your own position in life could be just as devastatingly uprooted someday; you forget that you are no better than the person trying to escape a country's war or tumultuous upheaval—just luckier. Now, in the midst of so much strife between people of different races, classes, religions, and (increasingly) political positions, we could benefit from Bapuji's insistence on humility.

Some try to show their humility and humanity by suggesting that we need to teach "tolerance" for each other. But I think that is coming at the problem from the wrong direction. What could be more condescending than "tolerating" someone else? The word signals that you see yourself as implicitly more deserving than others but will deign to accept them. I think Bapuji would say that tolerance is not only inadequate; it alienates us even more from each other. We can't absolve ourselves from the responsibility of truly understanding someone with a background unlike our own and being humble enough to accept and appreciate the differences.

Many Americans were shocked during the 2016 presidential election by the level of vitriol and hatred that one of the major party candidates spewed. He built an entire campaign by denigrating people and trying to convince his followers that if they stuck with him, they too could be better than those "others." His rantings reminded many of other tin-pot dictators around the world who have no real solutions for their people and live in an echo chamber of their own haughty conceit. This is not new—arrogant bullies have been causing harm and havoc in the world throughout history. Bapuji had to deal with many of them. He believed that those who scream the loudest often have the least to say. "Empty drums make the loudest noise," he told me once with a smile. Those who have real ideas, solutions, and integrity do not have to bang recklessly to be heard.

While I was at Sevagram ashram, Bapuji was involved in the very high-stakes struggle to gain India's independence from Britain. He opposed the compromise of partition, which involved dividing the country by cleaving off Pakistan as a separate state for Muslims. He knew that Muslim and Hindu families who were now living side by side would be uprooted and more violence would likely ensue. He sought equal rights also for women and the untouchables, who were often segregated in hamlets outside the cities and not allowed into temples or schools. Many political leaders told him the fight for equal rights was a distraction that could be dealt with once India was independent. But he insisted liberation for all could not wait. With his deeply felt humility, he knew that discrimination of any kind is an assault on our combined humanity.

When we look into a different culture and see people being oppressed, we immediately realize how wrong it is. Americans I meet often shake their heads in bafflement at the idea of India's untouchables. Why would the upper-caste Indians of the time have felt they would be polluted by letting the untouchables draw water from the same well? I gently remind them of the "whites only" signs that existed for years all over America in public bathrooms, drinking fountains, and swimming pools. Why indeed do we have these concerns? Perhaps it is our arrogance, telling us we are better than someone else. Or perhaps we have a secret foreboding that we really are *not* any better and so use the enforced separation to feed our egos and self-importance.

My grandfather understood that the lives and destinies of each of us are intertwined and that we need humility to recognize the truth of our interdependence. He brought this lesson to life one day when he asked me to bring my spinning wheel to his room. I came in and settled down, happy for what I assumed would be another session of talking and spinning with him. Instead he asked that I dismantle the spinning wheel. I was baffled, but I took the machine apart and sat with all the pieces spread out around me. I should have known by then that Bapuji always had a reason for what he asked. Now he suggested that I spin some cotton.

"How can I do that? The machine is dismantled."

"Very well, put it together again."

Slightly peeved by the waste of time, I got busy reassembling the machine. When I was almost done, he reached over and took a little spring that fit under the small wheel. He held it in his hand, clearly not planning to give it back to me.

"I can't put this together without the spring," I pointed out.

"Why not? It is just a tiny little part."

"Yes, but I need it for the spinning wheel to work."

"Oh, it's so small that it can't be of much consequence." He pretended to strain his eyes to see it in his hand. "Surely you can make the spinning wheel work without it."

"No, I cannot," I said firmly.

"Exactly," Bapuji said with joy in his voice. He waited for the lesson to sink in, and then he explained further. "Every part is important and contributes to the whole. Just as this little spring is necessary to make the spinning wheel work properly, so every individual is integral to the bigger society. No one is dispensable or unimportant. We work in unison."

Every part is important and contributes to the whole. Just as this little spring is necessary to make the spinning wheel work properly, so every individual is integral to the bigger society. No one is dispensable or unimportant. We work in unison.

In machines as in life, we need every part to be working in order for the wheels to spin smoothly. Bapuji's lesson could even be a key to business success. In big corporations, strong leaders understand that they are only as good as the people who work for them. If they have the humility to treat people at every level with respect and recognize each person's worth, their company is more likely to thrive. The huge retail chain Walmart recently decided to put this into effect by paying higher wages to all its workers. Walmart employs more people than almost any other private company in the world, so this was an expensive and bold step. The company would lose money in the short term but bet that treating people better would result in more loyal and harder-working employees. The early results were inspiring, as the stores began to function better and customer-satisfaction ratings soared.

Bapuji would not have cared much about Walmart's stock price or bottom line, but he would have been glad that in this case economic theory lined up with his humanitarian instincts. The person stocking the shelves in a store is like the spring in a spinning wheel: the whole can't function without him. Treating him well can make the whole enterprise more successful. An executive who has the humility to recognize each worker's value will succeed far better than one who arrogantly thinks that success depends only on the decisions she makes behind closed doors in her office.

On a bigger scale, we make a huge mistake when we dismiss large swaths of people, thinking they are not as important as we are. Even before the tragedy of 9/11 the world was shocked by young Muslims becoming suicide bombers. With no respect or regard for their own lives, they are willing to destroy themselves for what seems to them (however mistakenly) to be a bigger cause. Most of us are stunned by this attitude, which seems so alien to our understanding of the value of life. But it is possible that these young Muslims get the message that their lives don't matter from the larger society that ignores them and allows them to live in hopelessness and poverty. This in no way excuses their horrific actions, but it is a reminder that people who are discarded as unimportant may find dangerous ways to show their worth. If they can't contribute to making the spinning wheel work, they can smash it instead. The gun violence in some of America's worst neighborhoods has a similar source. When we ignore or demean certain racial or religious groups and tell people their lives are of little consequence to us, we are teaching them that their only power is to respond with violence.

In Bapuji's time and ours, the greatest human tragedies can often be traced to lack of humility and the huge inequalities that result. Wars are caused by arrogant and ego-driven leaders who want to extend their power and suppress or conquer others. Terrorism is committed by people who feel abandoned and forgotten. After a wave of police shootings of black men in America, the movement that arose called itself Black Lives Matter—and the name speaks volumes. People want to know they matter. Again and again we forget or refuse to accept that women, untouchables, Muslims, Hindus, Sunnis, Shias, Jews, Christians, immigrants, refugees—all matter. We need to stop being the kid on the playground who boasts "I'm better than you!" and realize how immature and foolish we sound when we take that approach. Bapuji insisted we should never be satisfied with a majority of people enjoying the good life. We must strive for *all* to enjoy the benefits of progress.

My grandfather started thinking about humility early in his life. As a child, he couldn't understand why he wasn't allowed to play with the son of the man who took away their garbage. (The man's job made the whole family "untouchables.") As he grew up, he saw how the British colonial power oppressed the Indian population, and eventually he faced the blatant bias of whites against nonwhites in South Africa. He realized that discrimination occurs when one group of people convince themselves they are better than others and so don't have to treat others with dignity. He believed the antidote was a big dose of humility.

Early in his efforts to get fair treatment for Indians in South Africa, Bapuji had a meeting with a government official who had been appointed to deal with the Indian issue. Bapuji told him that Indians weren't the problem that the South Africans depicted; they were, instead, hardworking and frugal people who contributed much to society. The official said he agreed and was on Bapuji's side. But he added that Bapuji needed to understand that the real issue of discrimination had a different basis. "It is not the vices of Indians that Europeans in this country fear but their virtues," he said.

It was an important lesson. When we repress people and deny them rights—whether women, minorities, or immigrants—we are choosing not to see their value. In putting them down, we make ourselves feel stronger. But it is a false strength. If we feel confident in ourselves, we appreciate other people's talents and abilities and want to encourage them when they're up and help them when they're down.

Bapuji cultivated humility and demonstrated his genuine strength by volunteering at a free hospital for the poor in Durban, South Africa. By nursing and tending the sick, he helped those who might otherwise be ignored. When the Boer War broke out shortly afterward, Bapuji used what he had learned at the hospital to organize an ambulance corps. He gathered more than a thousand Indian volunteers, many of them indentured laborers, who were quickly trained to tend to the wounded. The rocky ground where much of the fighting took place was too rough for the vehicles in those days, so Bapuji and his volunteers put the wounded soldiers on stretchers and carried them to the field hospitals. Often they walked twenty or more miles under a scorching sun. When the war ended, they were praised for their bravery, and the British awarded my grandfather a medal.

Bapuji was shocked at the inhumanity that war inspires. During the earlier Anglo-Zulu War, he had seen the British massacring the outnumbered native Zulus. "It was as if they were hunting for trophies," he said later. British soldiers armed with guns rode in on horses and attacked the natives fighting on foot with spears and sticks. Bapuji was appalled at the arrogance of power, how it can bring out the worst in people. When he led the ambulance corps in both wars, he treated everyone equally, aiding wounded Zulus as well as the British, insisting that all be treated with respect.

Bapuji's experiences in the wars convinced him that societies make a huge mistake when they accept a culture of violence as a means of asserting control and authority. True wealth doesn't come from money or dominance, but from appreciating that all people have dignity. "The good of the individual is contained in the good of all," Bapuji told me.

He also understood that much of the violence around the world is the result of what he called the Seven Sins of Society:

Wealth without Work
Pleasure without Conscience
Commerce without Morality
Science without Humanity
Knowledge without Character
Worship without Sacrifice (not of animals, but
    wealth)
Politics without Principles

Recently I added an eighth:

Rights without Responsibilities.

Once we understand that every life matters, we can use that to create change that benefits everyone. An Indian educator I much admire named Bunker Roy grew up attending the very best schools in India and was the country's national squash champion for three years. "The whole world was laid out for me. Everything was at my feet," he admitted. But instead of using his expensive and elitist education to become a doctor or diplomat, as his parents wanted, he decided to live in a poor village and dig wells. Roy approached the village with great humility. He didn't try to teach the elders; he wanted to learn from them. And so he began what became known as the Barefoot College, which uses the skills that people already have to let new ideas and possibilities emerge.

Roy based his approach on the principles my grandfather taught: equality and humility. As at Bapuji's ashram, Roy encouraged people to come for the challenge and opportunity to learn—not for money. At the beginning, he had people eat and sleep and work on the floor. Rather than telling the poor what they *should* learn, he decided to focus on what they already knew was important. Reading and writing weren't high on the list, but being able to have electricity in remote villages and pumps that brought water did matter. So he began teaching illiterate and impoverished women to become solar engineers. Their success was phenomenal. In just weeks, without having to study textbooks or read manuals, the women learned to gather solar power to light up the whole village. The women from the Barefoot College have now electrified towns and villages all over India. Other governments that have seen his incredible results have asked him to help them too, and he has spread his technique to Afghanistan and many countries in Africa. He likes to point out that illiterate grandmothers are now bringing solar power to Sierra Leone, Gambia, and other countries.

When Roy went to that first village, the elders wondered if he was running from the law or trying to escape a failed past. He had a hard time explaining that he believed the very poor had developed their own skills, which just needed to be brought into the mainstream. Because most of the women at his college were illiterate and they spoke different languages, he didn't bother with lectures or conversation; he used sign language and puppets to teach. He has joked that the puppets are made out of recycled World Bank reports. In other words, what great minds and institutions produce isn't necessarily better than the products of ordinary people. He runs the only college in India that won't hire teachers with a PhD or a master's degree; he relies on the knowledge that comes from people who work with their hands and understand the dignity of physical labor.

It takes great humility to say that even though you have attended the finest schools, you might be able to learn from an older woman who lives in poverty and can't read. Roy likes to quote my grandfather, who said, "First they ignore you, then they laugh at you, then they fight you, and then you win." He has won by sticking to principles of equality and collective decision making. Too often well-meaning outsiders come into a poor village with their own blueprints for change. Roy had the humility to recognize the knowledge and skills the people already had and help them develop further. He brought in technology that they could use and control.

***

First they ignore you, then they laugh at you, then they fight you, and then you win.

The success of Barefoot College proves that my grandfather's ideals of humility and his spirit of service can still bring about great changes in the world. It is also a reminder that we can create great things when we approach the world without arrogance.

My grandfather had an honest view of himself. However special he was in bringing change to the world, he didn't think he had been granted a special gift. "I have not the shadow of a doubt that any man or woman can achieve what I have if he or she would make the same effort and cultivate the same hope and faith," he said.

It's easy to *say* we appreciate everybody's worth, but much harder to actually practice. Most of the time we are convinced that we are right and are making the correct choices—which means that others are wrong. Psychologists have found that instead of gathering information and then making a decision, most people form a gut opinion and then look for the facts that will support it. We do this unwittingly in matters big and small. For example, if you're in the market to buy a new car, you'll first find one that you like, then look for reviews that support why your model is the best. We do this during elections too. Instead of carefully weighing all the facts, we pick a candidate to support, then focus on all the positive stories about him or her and ignore the negative.

I've had the experience in my own life of making a decision and being sure I was right, then finding out that real humility would require me to see the other side. Back in 1982 Richard Attenborough directed the movie *Gandhi*, based on the life of my grandfather. When I first heard that it was being made, I was quite worried. Attenborough decided not to consult any family members. Then I heard that the Indian government had spent $25 million to finance the movie—and I was horrified. I wrote a column for the *Times of India* criticizing the government and asserting that my grandfather would have preferred the money be used to help the poor. Twenty-five million dollars could have a huge impact on people's lives and shouldn't be wasted on a movie.

Shortly before *Gandhi* was released, I was invited to an advance screening. I sat down nervously in my seat, and almost immediately was moved to tears. The movie had some inaccuracies, but it captured the spirit of my grandfather brilliantly. It opened with a statement acknowledging that while it couldn't capture every event, it tried "to be faithful in spirit to the record and . . . the heart of the man." It accomplished that. I went home and wrote a follow-up column taking back my earlier criticism and admitting that I had only admiration and praise for the movie. In portraying my grandfather, actor Ben Kingsley would bring Bapuji's message of nonviolence and love to millions of people who would otherwise never hear it. *Gandhi* won eight Academy Awards, including for best movie, and Kingsley and Attenborough both won well-deserved Oscars.

And I got a great lesson in humility.

Bapuji wanted to get rid of the labels we use to describe each other and the distinctions we make in gender, nationality, and religion. He worried about patriotism as a way of trying to protect your own corner of the world without regard to anyone else's. When we barricade ourselves into rigid groups, we are saying that our way is better than any other and we want to insulate ourselves from seeing or hearing other positions. That path offers only divisiveness and violence. The nonviolent approach comes with enough humility to say that we respect other people's perspectives and passions, even if they are not the same as ours.

Letting go of labels and embracing other viewpoints isn't always easy, but the results can be powerful. A teacher in Rochester, New York, recently asked me to speak to her class about nonviolence, so I told the students about my grandfather's approach and his belief that treating people with love and respect and dignity could transform much of the anger and despair we face. After I left, the teacher asked the students to create a project using Bapuji's message in their daily lives. I came back a month later to hear the students present what they had devised. One heavy-set girl explained that her weight made her the butt of mean jokes and that she was often bullied. Usually she would react in anger and swear at the people who had been mean to her. But after hearing about Bapuji's approach, she decided to see how love would work instead. Whenever she was bullied, she responded with kind words—and the response so disarmed the bullies that they didn't know what to do. She began a club she called Hearts of Diamond and invited others at the school to resolve their conflicts by being loving rather than mean.

I was so impressed with this girl's project: she had landed on the important truth that bullies aren't as strong as they pretend to be—they are just looking for someone weaker so they can feel important. This young lady's technique allowed the bullies to lose their anger and feel embraced. Her pride contributed to theirs. Instead of railing and screaming and fighting to be at the top of some imaginary ladder, they could all feel good about being equals in loving respect.

Bapuji felt strongly that there must be fairness and respect in any civilized society. He accepted that there may not be full economic equality, but there should not be the enormous financial disparities that exist today. When successful members of society live in gated mansions and insulate themselves from the pain and agony of others, the imbalance can lead only to problems. We all like to take credit for our own achievements, but the truth is that nobody succeeds on his own. We need the humility to recognize and appreciate the contributions others have made to our prosperity.

A man I know named Rajendra Singh was trained as a medical doctor and eventually set up practice in the little village of Sariska, in one of the most arid regions of India. A few weeks into his practice an older man told him the villagers didn't need medicine or education nearly as much as they needed water. He invited the doctor to walk with him, and he showed him all the crevices in the rocky surfaces of the mountain range.

"The little rain we have flows into these crevices and disappears," the old villager explained. He shared some age-old wisdom of how to harvest water by digging small ponds for storage. That made sense to Dr. Singh, and he suggested the man lead the way in getting the project started. "I am too old, and the village people dismiss me as an eccentric," the man replied. "But you have degrees, so they would listen to you."

In the spirit of my grandfather, Dr. Singh decided to lead by example. He built a couple of ponds on his own land to catch the water flow, and when the rains came, the ponds filled up and the thirsty land around them began to soak up the water. The villagers were impressed and asked the doctor if he would help them dig more ponds. Before long, the arid land became fertile again, and the flow of water revived the community.

Dr. Singh then began helping other communities harvest water. He has already transformed more than a thousand square kilometers of arid land into an agricultural paradise. He points out that he didn't need to invent new technology or launch a multimillion-dollar project; he simply relied on knowledge that was already in the community. Seeing how the flow of water can transform an area reminded him that "flow" is essential in all our lives. As individuals, we flourish and bloom when we are connected as part of the flow of a larger community.

The humility that allows us to appreciate each other makes a stronger and more positive world—and gives resilience to each of us. As President Barack Obama was finishing his second term in office, he spoke about the many people who had been part of his achievements. He warned us against seeing ourselves as "just an assortment of tribes that can never understand each other" and urged instead that we recognize "one common humanity that can meet and learn [from] and love each other." My grandfather would have strongly agreed.

For all the knowledge and technology we have, we need the humility to realize that our education can continue for our whole lives. Astrophysicists doing leading-edge studies recently estimated that we have knowledge of only about 5 percent of the cosmos. That leaves 95 percent for us to learn about and explore. Our discoveries will come from many sources. We need the humility to rely on common villagers as well as great thinkers to expand our worldview. As my grandfather said, "Let the breeze of knowledge flow in from all the open windows."

Let the breeze of knowledge flow in from all the open windows.

The Five Pillars of Nonviolence

Most of us think of important people as being serious and imposing, but my image of my grandfather is of a kind, funny man who liked to relax and play games. At night at the ashram he liked to go out walking for a couple of miles, and I often got to accompany him. My grandfather was only about 5 feet 5 inches tall, and by the time I was fourteen, I was much taller than he. He would drape one arm around my shoulder and the other arm around a young man who joined us; he called us his "walking sticks." He would swing his legs off the ground when we least expected it and swing from our shoulders with the same delight as a little kid being swung by his parents and yelling, "Wheeeee!" If we slumped in surprise as he played his game, he would laugh and say, "You're not paying attention!"

Bapuji's robust sense of humor made him a down-to-earth man, and he used his natural wit to convince people that he wasn't very different from them. As he got older, people focused only on his noble qualities and assumed he had been saintly from birth. But he never claimed he had been born with any special talents and he reminded me often that he came from humble beginnings. He achieved his greatness only through determination and commitment. He was convinced that we can all change ourselves for the better if we want to.

Bapuji used fasting to make political statements, but when he was younger and hadn't yet started to simplify his life, he used food for a different purpose. He loved to eat, and one of his favorite foods was an Indian sweet bread called *puran poli*. One day in South Africa, he and my grandmother, whom we called Ba, invited some guests over for lunch. Ba was cooking in the kitchen when Bapuji wandered in, enticed by the good smells. He was delighted to see her making his favorite bread but told her worriedly, "We won't have enough for all the guests."

"This will be plenty," she said calmly.

"But I could eat all of this myself!" Bapuji insisted.

"No, you couldn't," my grandmother replied, shaking her head.

"Are you challenging me?" he asked with a twinkle in his eye. "Go ahead, make what you have, and let's see who's right."

My grandmother cooked up eighteen pieces of *puran poli*, each the size of a large pancake. She served them to my grandfather, who ate one after the other and polished them off happily. Ba had to admit defeat.

Over the years Bapuji gave up his beloved *puran poli* (maybe the eighteen pieces were enough for a lifetime!) and many other foods as his lifestyle became simpler and simpler. By the time I was with him at the ashram, his food was absolutely bland, with no salt or spices. Once I asked my relative Abha, who cooked his meals, to let me taste what she made for him.

"You won't like it," she warned me. "It's absolutely tasteless."

The concoction was a mush of vegetables cooked in goat's milk. I took a spoonful but could barely choke it down.

The next time I saw Bapuji, I asked him why he made himself eat such uninspiring meals.

"I eat to live, not live to eat," he said with a smile.

I've said that Bapuji wasn't perfect, and maybe he went a little too far with his simplicity. But he was making the point that if we learn to live simply, we can help others simply to live.

Bapuji believed in the power of personal transformation. Sometimes this requires great effort, and sometimes we just need the right nudge. He believed that small actions can snowball into much bigger ones. As usual he didn't lecture me about that; he let me learn it myself from his example and the stories he told.

One night at the spinning wheel as we sat comfortably together, he told me the story of a hopelessly disorganized young man who lived alone in a small apartment. The man never cleaned or did any household chores, and dirt covered everything. "His kitchen sink was overflowing with dirty dishes," Bapuji said. "Not just overflowing, but piled right to the ceiling!" The man knew his place was a pigsty, but he figured that if he didn't invite anyone over, then nobody would know.

At work one day he met a woman and started to fall in love with her. He took her on dates, but never to his apartment. They strolled in the park and talked by the river, and one day she plucked a beautiful red rose and gave it to him.

It was a gift of love, and even this man who allowed himself to live in squalor knew that it had to be preserved with dignity. He brought the rose home, and after rummaging through his dirty dishes, found a vase. He scrubbed it, filled it with fresh water, and put in the rose. Now he needed a place to display the vase, so he cleaned off the dining-room table. The vase looked pretty there, but he thought it would look even better if the rest of the room were as nice, so he put things away and polished the floor. Then he washed the dishes. The chain reaction of cleaning continued until his whole house was tidy and fresh. He wanted everything around him to be as beautiful as that rose. The woman's one small act of love in giving him a rose turned out to be life-changing.

Even as an awkward teenager, I was moved by that love story. All of us have our imperfections, but a simple gesture of tenderness can make us feel accepted and help us transform into a better version of ourselves. Sitting at that spinning wheel, I told myself fervently that as soon as somebody loved me, I would make sure I was worthy of her love. (And keep my house clean too.)

Bapuji agreed that love can have great power, but he wasn't just a romantic. He had an additional reason for telling that story. He wanted me—and all of us—to *be* roses in the world. We can each provide the bit of brightness and hope that can make people want to be better. One vivid example of love or hope or truth can make everything else seem dingy in contrast. Once that contrast is set, people around us have a clearer view of their own possibilities. They can be part of the dinginess or join in adding more roses to the vase. When you are good, you make everyone around you aspire to be better than they are.

One more point about the story: our sloppy bachelor cleaned up his act without anyone having to criticize him. He didn't have to be told that what he was doing was wrong—he already knew it. He just needed an example and an inspiration to make him happier doing dishes than leaving them in the sink. If the woman who gave him the rose had instead complained to him about his bad habits, he may never have changed. We respond better to positive incentives than negative ones. Telling a colleague, a friend, or a family member that he or she has failed or doesn't measure up will only backfire. People turn defensive and rebellious when attacked. But finding something to praise and admire will promote the behaviors you like and hope to encourage.

The example set by Bapuji's generous nature and kindly manner probably did as much to bring about change in India as anything he said or wrote. A positive spirit is one of the most powerful gifts we can give ourselves or others. Psychologists are now finding that when we express positive emotions like love, gratitude, and generosity, we dramatically increase our own sense of well-being and can even have positive effects on our health, including lowering blood pressure, decreasing stress, and sleeping better. Bapuji's nonviolent approach gave people a constructive and optimistic way to move forward in situations that might otherwise have seemed hopeless.

❈

People often think of my grandfather as uncompromising in his principles and willing to stand alone in his fight for justice. But some of the most insightful historians have pointed out that he was a negotiator first. One of his great skills was his empathy and understanding of his opponent's position. Bapuji started out trying to negotiate with the British government, staying respectful and calm when he did. But eventually he realized that negotiation wouldn't work and he needed a different approach. The peaceful Salt March was just one example of his moving to the next level. People in India who wanted to be free and independent were bursting with anger, and there were many violent and explosive incidents that took place all over the country. My grandfather gave them a positive way to voice their discontent and strive for change that would make things better. Nonviolence encourages the good and hopeful in people rather than the bitter and angry. My grandfather's calm demeanor and easy smiles reminded people that looking for peaceful opportunities is always better than getting mired in despair.

Some years after the Salt March, the British Parliament passed the Government of India Bill, which was a first step in bringing self-rule to 300 million Indians. Many considered it a great victory for my grandfather, but he wanted to be sure that his fundamental message of love and nonviolence was heard. His goal wasn't simply to replace one government with another; his *satyagraha* movement went beyond politics. A journalist at the time who opposed my grandfather's positions described a meeting he attended of some of the Indians who would take over from the British officials. He found them as arrogant and cold as the people they would be replacing. But he described Bapuji's expression as "one of extraordinary innocence and benignity, with two soft beams streaming out of his eyes." Though he disagreed with his positions, the journalist found himself spellbound.

The soft beams of light that streamed from Bapuji's eyes were a reflection of the genuine love and goodness and positive spirit he brought to everything he did. Remember that the word *satyagraha* that he used to describe his nonviolence movement translates as "soul force." You get strength from the positive and loving spirit you bring to your actions. He never saw his movement in strictly utilitarian terms. He wanted to convince the British to change their position, but he also wanted to bring a greater understanding and positive light to the world.

Bapuji saw that governments and religions often rule by fear. Religion controls people by threatening them with an angry God who will condemn them to hell if they misbehave. Those within a religious circle may also be judg-mental and cast out people who don't accept their views and demands. Governments can use more direct controls, like fines and imprisonment. Even parents and teachers, as we have seen, often rule by fear and threats of punishment.

Bapuji believed we need to move the world through love, not fear. He showed love and kindness and opti-mism, and people flocked to be around him.

Move the world through love, not fear.

My grandfather wanted people to understand the nuances of nonviolence well beyond avoiding physical aggression. He lived by the five pillars of nonviolence and he wanted me to try to follow them too. So I have tried to live my life with those five important foundations:

Respect
Understanding

Acceptance
Appreciation
Compassion

I sometimes hear people say that Bapuji had a utopian vision that can't exist in the real world. But I think quite the opposite is true. The principles he set out are absolutely basic to civilization, and we ignore them at our peril.

❀ ❀ ❀

Respect. Understanding. Acceptance.
Appreciation. Compassion.

Respect and understanding of other people, whatever their religion, race, caste, or country, is the only way the world can go forward. Putting up walls and divisions always backfires in the end, leading to anger, rebellion, and violence. In contrast, when we respect and understand each other, we naturally evolve to that third pillar, acceptance. The ability to accept other views and positions allows us to grow stronger and wiser.

The other two pillars of nonviolence—appreciation and compassion—help bring about personal happiness and fulfillment as well as greater harmony in the world. Appreciation has a very deep resonance and can make a profound difference in each of our lives. The happiest people aren't those with the most money but those who can appreciate the beauty and goodness around them. It's easy to find reasons to complain and criticize and point out what is wrong. We can give ourselves much more joy by choosing instead to look for things to appreciate every day.

Bapuji was masterful at appreciating the world around him. He looked for the good in everybody. Sometimes when I visit India, I meet children and families who have so much less than most Americans, yet they seem to appreciate what they do have so much more. I wonder if we dull our own abilities for appreciation by drowning ourselves in too much stuff. It's as if we spend our lives at an all-you-can-eat buffet and so can't see the pleasure in eating one shiny apple. Most of us aren't going to adopt the dramatic simplicity that Bapuji chose for his life, but we can use it as a model and a reminder that less is sometimes more. Less stuff and fewer distractions may lead to more appreciation and gratitude—and so more genuine happiness.

If finding reasons to be grateful doesn't come naturally, you can learn how in a few simple steps. Pause for a few minutes in the course of a day to appreciate a beautiful sunrise, a budding flower, or the sound of a child's laughter. Look at your life from the outside and think of all the people around the world who would be happy to be in your position. Make a list of the things you appreciate about your own family and friends. You can tuck it into a drawer to look at on those days when you need a reminder that gratitude comes from the inside, not the outside.

We do violence to ourselves when we focus on what we are missing or lacking rather than appreciating the gifts we have been given. You don't have to follow a particular religion or even any religion at all to appreciate the marvels and mysteries of the world—they are there for all of us. By bringing more appreciation into your life, you can change your attitude and your perspective on the world.

Too often we compare ourselves only to those who have more than us. But appreciating what we have leads to compassion for those who need our help. Compassion is much more than writing a check to a local charity (though that certainly helps). When you act from compassion, you stop to find out another person's strengths and hopes and figure out what you need to do to help him or her be independent. When you allow yourself to respond to others with compassion, you recognize their need for self-respect and treat everyone equally.

Once you understand others and incorporate them into your life, Bapuji's pillars of nonviolence will seem absolutely essential to the well-being and peace of each of us and the world as a whole. Imagine the happiness we could all feel and spread to others if we lived by those five pillars: respect, understanding, acceptance, appreciation, and compassion!

❧☙

Bapuji found ways to spread his message in even the most unlikely circumstances. Some years before I got to the ashram, my grandfather was attending one of the conferences in London to discuss the future of India. As always, he decided to wear the homespun cotton he had adopted as his uniform. He was representing the Indian people, most of whom lived in utter poverty, and the garments were a reminder of that. The British officials treated him with respect and arranged for him to stay in an elegant spot in London with security befitting a head of state. But Bapuji declined. "I'd like to live in the midst of the textile workers, preferably as their guest," he informed them.

The British officials were aghast. Remember that Bapuji's position on keeping Indian cotton in India had hurt the British textile industry. With Indians spinning their own cloth, British companies weren't able to charge the big markups that they had previously, and British workers were angry at my grandfather for their lowered wages.

"If you stay with the textile workers, they will kill you," one of the officials warned. "There is so much anger among them that we fear for your safety."

"That is all the more reason that I should stay with them—so that I can explain the case of the Indian people," Bapuji said calmly.

Reluctantly the British acceded to Bapuji's request, and he went to meet the textile workers. He approached them with the respect and understanding that were his hallmarks. He described to them the extreme poverty that was the norm in India and explained how spinning their own cloth allowed the people in some villages to rise above the most meager level of subsistence. He offered compassion for the British workers' plight and told them he understood that they too wanted to support their families in the best way possible. But he urged them to join him in helping the Indian people begin to climb out of poverty. Not only did the British textile workers listen respectfully to my grandfather, but he won their acceptance. Many became fans and supported his many endeavors.

It is unusual for angry people to change their position, and even more unusual for them to swing to a stance that goes against their own interests. But by listening and understanding, Bapuji managed to diffuse the textile workers' anger and give them a new point of view. He helped them see what was needed globally rather than just personally.

Bapuji's *satyagraha* movement is generally valued for its *reactive* nonviolence, when, in the face of an injustice like discrimination or bigotry, people band together to call attention to why it's wrong. They are reacting to a problem and trying to change it with passive or spiritual resistance. Besides my grandfather, Martin Luther King Jr. and Nelson Mandela and now many others have used this approach. They react to repression or exploitation with nonviolent protests. But Bapuji also believed in *proactive* nonviolence, which meant preparing the ground ahead of time for good actions to follow. If you plant the seeds of understanding and compassion, they will grow into sheltering trees that protect against wrongs raining down. So Bapuji cultivated the sensibilities and compassion of the textile workers as a kind of proactive nonviolence. He sprinkled the seeds of understanding. Without that, the workers might have erupted in violence and tried to repress or destroy the Indians seeking to raise themselves from poverty. Instead they came over to his side.

❦❧

My grandfather cared so deeply about his causes and spreading justice in the world that he could forget to have the occasional bit of frivolity and fun. Fortunately my grandmother was there to remind him. Ba had never learned to read or write, but Bapuji respected her wisdom. She sometimes challenged him about ashram life, and he was willing to listen. Bapuji didn't think his family should be treated any differently than anyone else at the ashram. But the first time I visited the ashram when I was very young, I discovered that Ba would sometimes make peanut brittle as a special treat and keep it hidden away to give to her grandchildren. Devoted as I was to my grandfather, I didn't mind getting a sweet snack from Ba now and then. She would smile slyly as she pulled out the candy, and we could enjoy a private moment together. Bapuji knew exactly what she was doing, but he never tried to stop her.

People all over India celebrated Bapuji's birthday on October 2, but he refused to allow any festivities at the ashram. He wanted to be treated like everyone else. While I was there, a group of women wrote to him asking to visit Sevagram and be part of his birthday lunch. He wrote back saying that the ashram would not be observing his birthday and anyway had no money to provide them with food. The women apparently felt strongly enough about celebrating his birthday that they arrived on October 2 just to be near him. At lunchtime, when all the ashram residents were congregated on the verandah of the dining hall, Ba noticed a group of ten women sitting under a nearby tree and getting ready to eat a lunch they had brought.

She went up to them and asked, "Why are you sitting here and not joining us for lunch?"

"Bapuji said the ashram can't afford to feed us and there would be nothing special on his birthday," one of the women explained.

"Oh, the old man forgets that we sometimes need to enjoy ourselves!" my grandmother exclaimed. "On his behalf, I am inviting you to come join us."

Bapuji welcomed Ba's views; in fact he urged all women to leave their kitchen and become equal partners in India's struggle for freedom. "As long as fifty percent of the population remains under subjugation, political freedom will be meaningless," he said.

That call for women's freedom was as radical as almost anything else my grandfather did. When he was a child, he had seen his own mother, Putliba, forced to hide her intellectual curiosity under veils of domesticity. Bapuji's father was the prime minister of one of India's large cities, and Putliba would have loved to participate in the discussions with the religious and political leaders who regularly came to their house. But women in India in the mid-1860s were expected to be as invisible as dutiful children. She couldn't come out while the men talked, so she would sit quietly in a nearby room and just listen, hoping to learn.

When my grandfather spoke at prayer meetings or in front of big crowds, he urged men to stop subjugating women and treating them like chattel. And he exhorted the women not to accept the myth that they were weak willed or needed to be protected. Too often people who are oppressed add to their own burdens by internalizing the negative images spread by those who seek to dominate them. He urged women to break out of that limiting mind-set and stand up to the men who tried to hold them down. "No one can liberate you until you liberate yourselves," he told them.

My grandfather insisted that men needed to "break the shackles of outdated tradition and learn to look at women with respect and dignity as equal partners." Though he held on to the old view that men were physically stronger and women spiritually stronger, his call for women to participate fully in public life was impressively progressive. Many political leaders told him that fighting for equality for women and "untouchables" was just a distraction and should wait until after Indian independence was achieved. But Bapuji stood strong in his belief that oppression from any source should not be tolerated even for a moment. The liberation of women and low castes could not wait.

Unfortunately it has waited. While women in most Western countries now have opportunities that my grandmother and great-grandmother could never imagine, there are still religions and cultures around the world that treat women with the same dismissiveness that Putliba faced. And too many women in more open societies still undermine themselves and don't have the courage to break out of old stereotypes.

Bapuji was right that the first step in liberation has to come from within.

You Will Be Tested

The two years I spent with Bapuji on the Sevagram ashram were a crucial time in both his life and world history. All the political forces in India were coming to a boil. The country was getting closer to achieving independence from Britain, but Bapuji's hope for a united country where people of all religions and castes could live together harmoniously was being dashed at every turn. An idea had been forged a decade earlier of creating a separate Muslim state out of some of India's northern provinces. The country would be called Pakistan, which means "Land of the Pure." Bapuji was ardently opposed to the partition.

One of the leaders of the partition movement was a Muslim named Muhammad Ali Jinnah. Like Bapuji, he had started his career as a lawyer in London, but he had never given up his proper (some would say "arrogant") bearing. He fought hard against Bapuji, so many people were shocked when, as independence drew closer, Bapuji proposed to Britain's Lord Mountbatten, the last viceroy of India, that Jinnah should become independent India's first prime minister. Bapuji thought this was the only way to win the trust of the Muslim minority and preserve a united country.

His suggestion was pretty spectacular when you think about it. American politicians care so much about staying in power that they are willing to stop legislation, stonewall Supreme Court appointments, and even shut down the government to feed their own egos and war chests. Bapuji was willing to say that the good of the country should be above all personal feelings and desires.

Lord Mountbatten later said he was "staggered" by the proposal, but that it wasn't the time for idealistic action. He needed to move forward with a steady plan. Nehru would become prime minister, and Jinnah the leader of Pakistan. Bapuji felt cut out of the complicated negotiations and headed to another part of the country to try to stop some of the bloody fighting between Hindus and Muslims that was leaving corpses scattered in the streets.

On June 3, 1947, negotiations came to an end and the agreement was signed: India was free of British rule, but it was now divided into two countries. The approaching partition sparked increasingly violent clashes between Hindu and Muslim radicals. Instead of joyously anticipating India's August 15 Independence Day, my grandfather was heartbroken. The mass disruption of the country was already starting. Ultimately the partition would lead to the largest migration in world history, with some 15 million people trying to escape the sectarian violence.

In early August, Bapuji made plans to head to other parts of the country to try to end some of the violence and bloodshed. People from Calcutta to Delhi feared that the religious massacres would intensify even further. I wanted to go with him on the trip, but for once Bapuji didn't agree. "It is not the place for young people," he told me.

So I stayed behind while Bapuji went to cities being torn apart by riots, whose residents were fearful of what would happen to them and their families after partition. He was stunned by the explosions of anger. When his train stopped in Calcutta, the local officials, afraid that the violence would get even worse, begged him to stay until Independence Day. He agreed, on the condition that he and the Muslim League's chief minister, Huseyn Shaheed Suhrawardy, sleep under the same roof.

"Adversity makes for strange bedfellows," he said. But instead of a joke, it was a masterful strategy. If the most famous Hindu in the world and the most prominent Muslim in the region could offer this show of unity, wouldn't the masses in the street respond by giving up some of their violence and bloodshed? They went together to a home that had been looted and stood empty in a neighborhood destroyed by ethnic fighting. At first my grandfather was surrounded by angry mobs, and he thought the furious people would kill him. But his calm words with Suhrawardy at his side had an astonishing effect.

On August 15, instead of more horrific killing in Calcutta, people marched through the streets chanting "Hindus and Muslims are brothers!" People in the crowds threw rose petals at my grandfather. Lord Mountbatten congratulated Bapuji on "the miracle of Calcutta" and admitted that he had established an oasis of peace where the military had failed. Amid all the turmoil and bloodshed, it was a great statement on the power of nonviolence.

Meanwhile, across the country in Delhi, the new prime minister raised the flag of a free India for the first time.

"If credit is due to any man today it is to Gandhiji," he told the huge cheering crowd.

I was with my family that day in Bombay. Millions of people came out to march in parades and dance in the streets, but out of respect for my grandfather, none of our extended family participated. "I don't see any reason to rejoice," Bapuji had said.

Some of us children and teenagers went out to see the lights and hear the noise. I remember being torn by the excitement all around me and the sadness I had seen in Bapuji's eyes when he realized that his plea against partition would not be heeded. His colleagues had abandoned him in their rush to get into power. He saw partition as the negation of all he stood for; it would encourage more divisiveness between people and—as was quickly becoming obvious—would lead to an unprecedented massacre of innocent people on both sides.

In the following days Bapuji continued to visit one village after another, pleading for sanity and peace. But even he couldn't hold back the roaming gangs who began killing again. Panicked refugees fled in all directions. There were reports from one town that the line of people trying to escape on foot stretched over fifty miles. Bapuji made his way to Delhi and maintained his calm demeanor even as the violence moved closer and people in Lord Mountbatten's own house were murdered. The mayhem and upheaval in the country were tragic proof to my grandfather of what happens when nonviolence and *satyagraha* are forgotten.

❀❀❀

With so much uncertainty in the country, my parents thought it was time for us all to return to South Africa. In those days the sea voyage from India to South Africa took twenty-one days, sometimes longer. The first passage we could get was in early November, nearly three months away.

Father wrote Bapuji of the plan, and he sent his blessings to all of us. Then he sent some special words to me. "Do not forgot what I have taught you, Arun," my grandfather wrote. "I hope you will continue working for peace when you grow up."

---- ❀❀❀ ----

I hope you will continue working for peace
when you grow up.

I had learned so much in our two years together, and I stood a little taller at his words of encouragement.

I didn't realize they were the last he would ever give me.

❧✤☙

In the two years that I had been with Bapuji, he had been a positive and transforming force in India—and he had inspired similarly dramatic changes in me. I no longer felt angry all the time, and when I was angry, I knew how to redirect it to do good. I could be the positive spark of electricity in the world. I had learned the nuances of nonviolence, and just as Bapuji hoped, I wanted to dedicate myself to fighting bigotry and discrimination and all the inequalities that lead to violence in the world.

The journey home was long, but it wasn't as harrowing as our arrival. I smiled when I remembered my exhausting walk that first day from the Wardha train station to Sevagram. Now as I was leaving, I was still a teenager with much to prove to myself and others, but I would never again let my ego rule my common sense. I had learned about humility and that you prove yourself by your heart and your actions.

Back in South Africa at last, my parents told me that a school had opened for the Indian community just a few miles from where we lived on the Phoenix ashram. I never had to go to the terrible convent school again or deal with the punitive nuns. My sister Ela and I began to attend together rather than traveling the seventeen miles into the city each day. All that was good, but it still felt strange to be back in South Africa. I had become an entirely new person in two years. My parents' home on the Phoenix ashram offered more comforts than I'd had at Sevagram—and better food. But my heart was still in India with my grandfather, and I thought often about going back.

But a reunion would never occur. On January 30, two months after I left him, the unthinkable happened.

Ela and I were walking home from school, making our way along the muddy track created by the trucks and tractors of the farmers working the land. It was a hot day and tall sugarcane surrounded us. We hadn't gotten very far when Ela protested that she couldn't go any farther. With a sigh, she sat down on the ground. "I'm not walking anymore. You'll have to carry me," she demanded.

Before my education from Bapuji, I would have tugged her along or gotten angry at her childishness. (She was six years younger than I.) But now I knew to handle the situation with respect and understanding.

"I am not carrying you, so I will just have to leave you here," I said calmly.

I wasn't really going to leave her, so I simply stood. That's when I noticed an older man who lived in our Phoenix ashram walking rapidly toward us. He almost never left the ashram grounds, so I was very surprised to see him. I wondered where he was headed. It took me a moment to realize that he was coming in search of us.

When he got close he called out to me with panting urgency: "Arun, run home immediately. Your mother needs you. I will bring your sister."

"I am already heading home. What's the rush?" I asked.

"Just go. Run. Don't argue. Your mother needs you."

I realized something very serious had happened. I ran home and found my mother on the phone, heaving with sobs. She hung up when I came in, but the phone rang; she answered it but could barely speak.

In between the tears and phone calls, she managed to sputter out the horrible truth she had just learned.

My beloved grandfather had been murdered.

"We will never see him again," my mother cried.

I was stunned. I asked where my father was.

"He went to town this morning for a meeting, and I don't know how to get in touch with him."

She kept trying to talk to me, but the phone kept ringing and ringing as more people heard the news and called to share their horror and dismay. I stood in the midst of the cacophony and began to weep. All the moments of the two years I lived with him flashed in my mind. Racing at the spinning wheel, swinging him from my shoulder, the caress of his hand on my cheek when I tried to make him laugh. It was not possible that he was gone.

"How could anyone kill Bapuji?" I asked my mother.

I knew that there had been many assassination attempts on him in the past, often by right-wing Hindus who thought he had betrayed them. But he had survived them all. I thought he was indestructible.

My father soon arrived home, ashen and holding back his tears. He had finished his meeting and been in the market buying fruit when he heard the awful news. Some of the vendors had offered to drive him home, but my father had managed to keep his composure and get back to us. He hugged my mother and held us close.

The house became more and more chaotic as close friends learned of the assassination and came over. "Is it really true?" each would ask.

My father tried to reach his brother in India to get more details, but it took a while to get through. Telecommunications were primitive where we lived, and the call had to be placed through a series of operators. When we did get connected, the line was shaky, but my father managed to convey that we wanted to come for the funeral. My uncle said there was no time. Bapuji was assassinated at 5:16 in the evening, and within a few hours nearly a million people had descended on Delhi. Officials feared that if they delayed the funeral, half of India would turn up and there would be riots. My uncle had agreed to arrange the funeral for the following afternoon. We would have to say good-bye from five thousand miles away.

The next day, along with my parents, I listened to the funeral proceedings over a crackling radio. I learned that my grandfather had been staying at Birla House in Delhi, the same place I had once stayed with him. He had strolled into the garden to lead a prayer meeting with his grandnieces at his side as his "walking sticks." As the crowd parted for him, a man rushed forward and pushed aside the woman next to my grandfather—the place where for the last two years I could most often be found. He shot Bapuji three times.

Many world leaders wanted to attend the funeral, but like us, they weren't able to arrive in time. The pope sent a tribute, as did President Harry Truman and King George VI. More than a million and a half Indians of every religion, caste, and color joined the funeral procession; likely the same number watched from vantage points around the city. Perhaps the most stunning tribute was when the violence in India came to an abrupt halt. Someone described it as being like the throwing of a switch. At the news of his death, the rampant killing ended—and suddenly Bapuji's dream of peace and unity seemed possible after all.

But for me, listening to the radio commentary from thousands of miles away didn't bring any peace at all. I tried to envision what was happening, and my initial shock and sadness turned to anger. As we clustered around the radio, I finally exploded.

"If I had been at Birla House, I would have throttled the person who shot Bapuji! I would have killed him!" I said furiously.

My father wiped tears from his eyes and looked at me with great seriousness. "Have you already forgotten the lessons your grandfather taught you?" he asked quietly. He was sad, but I heard the great compassion in his voice. Then, as Bapuji would do, my father pulled me to him. "Did he not say we must use anger intelligently? What would be the best use of the anger you feel now?"

I thought for a moment and took a deep breath. "To work like he did to stop violence in the world."

My father nodded. "That's right. Never forget his lessons. The best thing we can all do for Bapuji is to continue his mission and dedicate our lives to seeing that tragedies like this don't happen again."

My father knew that I needed an outlet for my anger, and positive action can often push away negative thoughts. We decided to plan our own memorial service to help ourselves as well as the legions of mourners in South Africa. My father suggested we put together a special memorial issue of the *Indian Opinion*, started by Bapuji and continued as a weekly by my father. We got people to share memories and photographs with us, and we researched my grandfather's life. Within a month we had a special hundred-page commemorative issue, printed on a primitive hand-operated press. The project redirected our minds from grief and anger, demanding instead our love and warm attention.

I looked with pride at the issue we created and turned the pages over and over, thinking about my grandfather. But I couldn't stop myself from replaying the shooting in my mind and imagining myself at Bapuji's side. Could I have stopped the gunman?

"I wish I could kill that murderer right now," I told my parents one day.

My mother sighed. She knew how I felt, but she also knew that my grandfather would not appreciate the sentiment. "Your grandfather would want you to forgive the person who did this," she said quietly.

Her words caught me up short. Of course that was what Bapuji would have wanted. Instead of offering forgiveness to the killer, I wanted revenge. But I knew Bapuji would say that revenge is never the right solution. A desire for revenge eats away at you, destroying your peace of mind and leaving you constantly on edge. Instead of hurting you once, the evildoer takes over your life and destroys you again and again. I couldn't let that happen—or I would be letting Bapuji down.

Bapuji had taught me that nonviolence was not the same as passivity or cowardice. It's acceptable to use limited force to disarm aggressors and protect the ones you love. If I had been one of his "walking sticks" that day, Bapuji would have wanted me to tackle his would-be killer and not just run away. But I hadn't been there. And now the question was how to respond to what had already occurred.

"Forgiveness is more manly than punishment," Bapuji had said.

***

Forgiveness is more manly than punishment.

When we are tested, we don't prove our strength with violence or anger but by directing our actions for good. India had given Bapuji the great gift of a brief peace after his death. I had to give him the similar gift of forgiveness in the face of great evil. Bapuji had once explained that it is easy to love those who love you, but the real power of nonviolence comes when you can love those who hate you.

"I know how difficult it is to follow this grand law of love," he had said. "But are not all great and good things difficult to do? Love of the hater is the most difficult of all. But even this most difficult thing becomes easy to accomplish if we want to do it."

I know how difficult it is to follow this grand law of love. But are not all great and good things difficult to do? Love of the hater is the most difficult of all. But even this most difficult thing becomes easy to accomplish if we want to do it.

He was right that it was difficult to find forgiveness, but I knew I had to do it—both for myself and for him. It would be my tribute to our two years together. I remembered again how my grandfather liked to say that an eye for an eye just makes the whole world blind. We need to redefine what we mean by justice. Our goal after a tragedy should be to see how we can make the world better, not to prove that we can descend into more violence and revenge.

And so in the years since my grandfather died, I have dedicated myself to spreading his messages of forgiveness and hope and nonviolence.

❧✦❧

Unfortunately tragedies continue. With every senseless murder in America, my adopted country, friends and family members are left with the same torment and pain that I experienced that day by the radio.

I spent many years grappling with the question of how we should respond to unthinkable acts. In 1999 more than a dozen students were killed at Columbine High School in Colorado, in what was then the deadliest school shooting in American history. A friend of mine in the area asked that I speak to the survivors. Everyone was angry and wanted vengeance. Shortly before the meeting, my friend asked me what I intended to say.

"I will talk about forgiveness and moving on with their lives," I replied.

"If you do that, they'll throw you out of the room," he warned me. "They are too angry to hear that."

But I stood up before the group and spoke about nonviolence and shared the lessons of forgiveness I had learned from my parents and grandparents. I told them I understood their pain and anguish because I had experienced it. I urged them to move ahead and try to fill their hearts with love instead of hate because it was the only way to a better society. Instead of being thrown out of the auditorium, I got a standing ovation.

More recently, in 2014, I found myself once again addressing a crowd of mourners. This time it was in Ferguson, Missouri, after the killing of an eighteen-year-old black man by a white police officer led to charges of racial discrimination. A huge group had gathered to show their solidarity, and they read aloud the names of the 110 people murdered in Ferguson that year. There was anger in the crowd, and the speakers emphasized the need for whites to acknowledge the prejudices they wittingly or unwittingly harbored against blacks.

With all the finger-pointing about who was in the wrong, I suddenly felt as though I were back at my mother's side, hearing her tell us children, "When you point a finger at someone, you have three fingers pointing back at you." Instead of looking for what others have done wrong, we need to look at ourselves.

When it was my turn to speak, I tried to channel Bapuji and find a positive outlet for the crowd's anger. I wanted to help them heal, but I also challenged them to move beyond vengeance. "Prejudice exists in every one of us, whatever our color or race," I said. "Unless we are willing to recognize this weakness in our character, we will never change. We transform the world only when we face challenges with love and kindness rather than hatred and meanness."

I shared with them Bapuji's most important words: *We must be the change we seek.* I saw nods in the crowd and murmurs of understanding. I was moved that these grieving people could still be touched by Bapuji's powerful message and understand his call to look beyond labels and find the good in everyone.

The power of my grandfather's lessons can inspire all of us in good times and bad, and his light of hope will continue to shine. If we want this world to change, we have to change ourselves.

If we want peace in the world, we have to find peace in ourselves.

Lessons for Today

My grandfather's murderer was a right-wing Hindu who was outraged by Bapuji's philosophy of erasing the caste system and bringing equality to all. Others in his mold continue to try to undermine my grandfather's memory. They disagree with his message that there is good in all religions and that we need to recognize and support all beliefs. "Religions are different roads converging upon the same point," Bapuji said. "What does it matter that we take different roads so long as we reach the same goal?"

Bapuji looked for fundamental truths and urged people to read all the scriptures and find the positive points in each. People with narrower viewpoints want to believe that only their position is correct. They try to boost themselves by undermining others. They are afraid to be challenged and attack those who offer a wider view. Bapuji would have told them that such cowardice is not a sign of faith.

In speaking of my grandfather, Albert Einstein famously said, "Generations to come will scarce believe such a man as this ever walked upon this earth." U.S. Secretary of State George C. Marshall called him "the spokesman for the conscience of all mankind." One commentator said my grandfather proved that humility and simple truths are more powerful than empires. Bapuji had no title or wealth or official office. He didn't rule an army or an empire or discover the theory of relativity. But he spoke truths that we understand deep in our hearts. Perhaps that is why his name and image have been so revered.

In the time I spent with him at Sevagram ashram, Bapuji had me make a list of my weaknesses and bad habits—not to berate myself, but so I would know what

I needed to improve. You need to know your weaknesses, he explained, to be able to transform them into strengths. Your goal every day is to be better than you were the day before. Once you start trying to improve, there's a snowball effect. I've continued that approach my whole life. Bapuji taught me that my purpose is to make a positive impact on the world, and I consciously strive to do things that matter.

When I first moved to America, I wanted to share Bapuji's philosophy with college students. Since I didn't have a PhD, universities wouldn't allow me to teach. Bapuji never let formalities like that get in his way—he always found his own path. So I started a nonviolence institute in my grandfather's name and began giving informal workshops and lectures. Working on an individual level to help people gain a better understanding of justice and conflict resolution, I saw how powerfully Bapuji's ideals still resonated. His philosophy helps bridge the gaps between people.

At one point in the early 1990s, anger about police brutality and racial injustice sparked riots in Los Angeles. I was living in Memphis, which suffered a similar incident and also seemed about to erupt, and people in the community asked me to intervene to calm the tension. I wasn't completely sure what to do. I didn't have my grandfather's magnetism or ability to persuade people. But I knew that whenever he couldn't find an answer, he organized a prayer service and invited people to look for answers with him.

The incident in Memphis boiled up on a Thursday, and I decided to hold an interfaith service on Sunday. I spoke to the board of the university where my institute was located, and they said it would take at least two weeks to prepare for an event like that. Two weeks! I pointed out that if your house is burning now, you can't wait two weeks to find the water supply.

So I gathered a small group of colleagues, and we personally called all the religious organizations in Memphis. We asked each of them to come and offer a five-minute prayer of peace and harmony. I didn't care how big or important they were—they all had the same five minutes.

That Sunday more than six hundred people gathered on a football field we had chosen for the service. I think it helped that it was a neutral ground—not a church or mosque or synagogue—so no particular tradition dominated and everybody felt equal and respected. More than thirty religious groups came forward to offer their five-minute prayer of peace. An incredible feeling of connection and friendship and understanding floated between the goal posts of the football field that day. People who once thought they had very little in common smiled and hugged each other. The spiritual atmosphere lingered and had a calming effect for weeks after. Many said the prayer service saved Memphis from exploding in violence.

Peace and hope can blossom when we open ourselves to others. In joining together we flourish in ways we never can if we stand alone. When I was at the ashram with Bapuji, he insisted that we look beyond our immediate relatives and accept all of humanity as family. Just as you would be willing to make personal sacrifices to help a brother or sister in distress, you should be willing to feel the pain of neighbors and even strangers and make similar sacrifices to help them. At first it bothered me that Bapuji wouldn't make concessions for me. I was his grandson—didn't that make me more special than anyone else? Only later did I understand the much bigger message he was sending: too many of us spend our time trying to protect our own small part of the world; we forget that we are all interconnected and can't flourish by ourselves.

You give yourself and the world a great gift when you choose to take a wider view and look for commonalities rather than differences. We each survive only if the rest of the world survives. The rich are getting richer, and the poor are just made poorer. If you are in the first group, that may seem just fine to you. But as we continue to support the stark division between rich and poor, we invite conflicts to occur over and over. And we hurt ourselves (and the world) in other ways too. Consider, for example, that because the poorest people in Asia, Africa, and Latin America don't have fuel for cooking, heating, and washing, they are chopping down whole forests for wood to burn. In the process all of us suffer from the damage to the environment. We are all connected. When 20 percent of the world's population use 80 percent of the world's resources to maintain their level of affluence while 80 percent of the population are left to scrounge for a livelihood, it is a recipe for disaster.

Americans are making a dangerous mistake in believing that we can protect our own interests by walling ourselves off from others. We expect that military might will win the day in any conflict, so we spend almost 60 percent of the federal budget on the military and weapons of mass destruction. We build more weapons than we can use and then sell them around the world. The United States has already demonstrated that it is a superpower in military strength. It now needs to show the world that it can be a superpower in moral strength. That means being willing to do what is good for the world and not just what is to our own advantage.

When the horrors of 9/11 occurred, America responded by bombing Iraq, which ultimately led to more and expanded violence in the Middle East. Once

Americans accepted that Iraq and 9/11 were truly unrelated, we rallied behind a war against "terrorists" that has been going on for many years now, with no end in sight. Instead of getting calmer, the world seems to become more dangerous, with terrorist attacks in Paris and Brussels and throughout the Middle East.

People ask me often, *What would Gandhi do against terrorism?* I think my grandfather would have urged a foreign policy based in compassion rather than greed. He would have explained that our relationships with the rest of the world are founded in mutual respect, understanding, and acceptance. Immediately after 9/11 he might have asked Americans to try to understand the source of hate and frustration that caused people to attack us in the most devastating way. "Hold on!" some Americans might say. "We didn't do anything wrong. We were the ones attacked." That is absolutely correct. But if there is hatred brewing in the world, we should try to stop it. My grandfather would have reached out to those nations and people angry at the United States to try to improve our relationships. "You cannot breed peace out

of non-peace," he once said. "The attempt is like gathering grapes of thorns or figs of thistles." Humility heals
wounds; arrogance aggravates them.

I think my grandfather would look with dismay at
many of the current world leaders who seem more intent
on enriching themselves than on bettering the lives of
the people in their countries. He believed ardently that
people in power should use their position for the good
of their fellow men and women. But he knew that didn't
always happen. "Power comes from sincere service.
Actual attainment often debases the holder," he said.
Many people in government now focus only on winning
elections and advancing their own careers, and they are
willing to spew hatred and bigotry to get their way. They
don't seem to care that they are undermining the very
government and democracy they are meant to serve.

So how do we stand up to the wrongs and injustices
and outrages we see every day? First, we truly have to
see them. I think back to that day in South Africa in
1895 when a white man decided he didn't want to share
a compartment with someone of darker skin, and he got

the police to throw my grandfather off the train. It was Bapuji's first experience with blatant prejudice, and he was stunned. But when he told other Indians what happened, many of them just shrugged. If the white people didn't want him in first class, why didn't he just move to another car? "Because it is unjust," Bapuji said repeatedly. "We cannot accept injustice meekly."

But the apathetic responses also made him realize that "nobody oppresses us more than we oppress ourselves." We stop noticing the wrongs that are done to us and inflicted on others. Preoccupied with our daily lives and a desire to get along, we stop paying attention. Outrageous behavior starts to seem normal.

Bapuji would tell us all—right now!—to wake up to the inequities and injustices of the world. We don't have to accept bigotry and unfairness. We must fight it on all levels. In encouraging people to take action, though, Bapuji recognized that there is no point in fighting hate with hate or anger with anger. Doing that only multiplies the very problems we want to eliminate. He believed change could come only from positive approaches—from love, understanding, self-sacrifice, and respect.

My grandfather's work for change started with an invitation to dialogue. When that failed, he would embark on a massive public protest to gain the sympathy of people on all sides of the issue.

The kind of nonviolent protests Bapuji encouraged could work today, but we have to think about our ultimate goals and what we are trying to achieve. For example, the rampant police shootings of young African American men are atrocious and must be condemned. But the protests that followed each one often focused only on the need to punish the culprits. Bapuji would have urged taking a longer view. People do indeed need to be held accountable, but the greater purpose of the community should be to erase the underlying fears and prejudices that led to the shootings. Otherwise those fears and prejudices remain intact (even if suppressed) until the next occasion, when they erupt again.

Maybe a better approach would be to try to understand implicit bias and see how even the most well-meaning among us can slip up. At our M.K. Gandhi Institute for Nonviolence, one of our diversity workshops had an unusual twist. The person running it had made masks out of photographs of people of all races. At the workshop, each of us was handed a mask to put on and told to look in the small mirror placed in front of us. It was startling to look through the eyes of the mask into the mirror and see a stranger. We were given two minutes to describe the person we had become.

All of us in the workshop were thoughtful people from upper-middle-class backgrounds and represented many different races. We were confident that we had no prejudices—and every one of us was proven wrong. Latent stereotypes emerged in the descriptions we gave. Confronted with an unfamiliar face, we fell back on expectations based on race or gender or age.

My background in South Africa, where I suffered prejudice of the worst kind, had made me understand its dangers, and my years with Bapuji had convinced me of the need to fight prejudice on every level. But at the workshop that day, I realized I could be as guilty as anyone else of measuring people by how they looked.

Bapuji's goal was to transform society and make us see our commonalities rather than our differences. Many groups now take a different course and use disruption as an end in itself. They are willing to paralyze communities to make society aware that they exist and deserve respect and recognition. They don't want understanding or acceptance—but to live on their own terms. I have deep sympathy for their plight, and I know how difficult the battles can be. But no society has survived under a "divide and rule" policy. A divided country or community eventually falls apart. And that is truer now than ever.

Many leaders would like to close doors and pretend that the world outside their borders doesn't exist or doesn't matter. But the world is shrinking and societies are becoming more, not less, multiracial and multireligious. Bapuji saw that change and understood that we should not strive to live among our own ethnic or racial group and join the mainstream only for business or commercial activity. Rather, we need to live and work with shared views of what is good for all of us.

America has fallen into a spiral of identity politics, where people live in separate communities and voting lines are drawn to encourage those distinctions. Many people vote not for what is good for the entire country but for what they perceive to be good for their group. (Ironically the person or party they think will support their interests often doesn't.) Real equality happens when we can step outside our small group and look at the greater good. True democracy ensures that everyone is not only equal but embraced and respected.

Bapuji pointed out that politicians "often have a trick of wrapping Truth in a veil of mystery and giving to what is temporary and unimportant preference over the permanent and deeply important." I wish his reminder could be emblazoned on every voting booth. Political campaigns get caught up in personal issues or false promises, and the bigger worldview and what really matters are pushed aside. People suffer and countries fall apart from this shortsightedness.

❊❊❊

Politicians often have a trick of wrapping Truth in a
veil of mystery and giving to what is temporary and
unimportant preference over the permanent and
deeply important.

As an example, Berlin has erected potent memorials to the Holocaust and the Jews who were killed out of meaningless hatred. Posters near the main square show how the city was devastated at the end of World War II, with German citizens of all religions left huddling without food and shelter. So many innocent people of varied backgrounds and dreams died or suffered from the fallout of hatred. The memorials should give us hope that we have learned from the past.

But have we really changed? Have we learned the lessons of past devastations? A Nazi-type hatred of diversity continues in countries around the world, and it is the most dangerous problem we have. We see its vicious results every day, in bullying in schools and harassment on the streets and in mass killings and global displacement. Even since World War II hate has fueled genocides in Cambodia, Rwanda, and Bosnia. Right now we are witnessing the destruction of Syria. The horror may seem far away, but many of the people who have lost everything are people just like you and me: they want to do meaningful work, to feed their families, to raise their children in safety, to support their communities, to live in peace. Now they are living in refugee camps and wondering why nobody seems to care or wants to help them.

Once we recognize what we have in common rather than what separates us, we approach the world and each other with a different perspective. You might think a current conflict or a recent tragedy doesn't affect you, but today's in-group can be the out-group tomorrow. Once we start dividing people—by race, religion, nationality, gender, sexual preference, political view, body type, age, socioeconomic status, ability or disability, language, accent, personality type, favorite sports team—there is no end to the distinctions that can be made. Ultimately we all are outsiders to someone else!

Hatreds and discriminations that occur far away from us can be confusing. I have spoken to many Americans who admit that the distinction between Hutus and Tutsis in Rwanda, between Shia and Sunnis in the Middle East, and even between Muslims and Hindus in India are a bit mysterious. To an American of Judeo-Christian background, each pairing seems to be more alike than different. Yet each has tried to destroy its counterpart.

I mention this not to mock Americans' ignorance of world religions but to point out how appropriate the confusion really is. Often the people we discriminate against are the ones who are most like us. The loyalties we form for our own group—and the disdain we have for outsiders—often make no sense at all. Psychologists have found that when people are randomly assigned to a particular group, they immediately prefer it and insist that it is better than the others. That's true no matter how unimportant the distinction that's being made. Give some people red T-shirts and others blue T-shirts, and alliances will form. Experiments have shown that the people wearing the red T-shirts will be nicer and more supportive to their fellow red shirts than to people in blue (and vice versa, of course). We are more likely to help and cooperate with the people we consider "us" than those we think of as "them."

Psychologists are now looking at the sources of this "in-group bias." Some think we are intrinsically wired to prefer the group where we find ourselves. But we also teach our children certain cultural norms and expectations, and certainly an educational system that encourages inclusiveness rather than divisiveness can start to make a difference. The equality and inclusiveness I learned from Bapuji have remained a powerful part of my life over all these decades—and will remain so. We can try to teach those lessons to our own children, whatever the outside influences pulling them in a different direction.

Many of the problems that divide and destroy us cannot be solved by legislation. They can be solved only by a willingness to open our minds and hearts to understand and respect each other. If he had been here, my grandfather would have had a big smile in 1964 when President

Lyndon Johnson signed the Civil Rights Act, giving equal rights to people regardless of race, religion, sex, or national origin. He would have been equally pleased by the follow-up legislation four years later, promising fair housing for all. But he would have been wise enough to know that it was just a start. He would not have been surprised that now, more than fifty years later, lack of equality still exists.

People have to believe change is possible. Five years after the Civil Rights Act of 1968 was made into law, the Justice Department brought a legal suit against a realty company in New York that it said was discriminating against potential tenants and refusing to rent to African Americans. The president of that realty company was Donald Trump. The legislation didn't stop his discriminating, and years later many voters didn't seem to care. He is now the president of the United States.

The civil rights legislation moved America halfway forward—but we stopped there. The other half of the way needs to be traversed through soul-searching, enlightenment, and education. The same can be said about legislation giving rights to women and gays and lesbians. Changing laws to protect people is vital, but the real change comes when people see the harm that prejudice causes, admit the wrongs they have done in the past, and embrace others rather than shun them.

Bapuji said often that a society cannot be measured by a material yardstick but only by the depth of its love and respect for all. He often referred to the Sanskrit word *sarvodaya*, which means "welfare of all." He believed *everyone* has the right to decency, happiness, and freedom from want. We are all at least partially motivated by self-interest, and he understood that. But instead of focusing exclusively on ourselves, we would all feel better and worthier if we looked beyond our own needs and desires. Bapuji used the word *swaraj* to describe the freedom that all people deserve—and that we have to help each other achieve. He spoke of it as more than just political freedom; he yearned for "*swaraj* for the hungry and spiritually starving millions."

Bapuji had a very simple test for deciding whether or not an action was right. He said that whenever you were in doubt you should "recall the face of the poorest and weakest person whom you have seen, and ask yourself if the step you contemplate is going to be of any use to her or him." Will it help that person gain control of his or her life, dignity, or *swaraj*? If so, he said, "you will find your doubts and yourself melt away."

Whatever is happening in politics or the greater world, we can each still have an influence. Every time I go to India, I am overcome by the extent of the poverty—and then equally overcome by the determination of many individuals to change lives and lift up the most needy.

A woman I met many years ago named Ela Bhatt began arranging microloans to women to start small businesses, such as selling fresh fruits and vegetables. Over the years the program encompassed more than 9 million women in all parts of India. After a while some of the women told Ms. Bhatt they were not happy depending on the commercial banks for their microloans; they suggested starting their own cooperative. She kindly explained how difficult that would be. Most of the women were illiterate and couldn't even sign their own names. "We want to learn!" they told her.

So, with the women gathered in her living room, she began an impromptu class that lasted all night. The next morning she gathered the necessary forms and watched proudly as each woman signed her name to the incorporation papers. They dubbed themselves the Self-Employed Women's Association and soon launched the SEWA Cooperative Bank. It has since become a flourishing institution that helps poor women become more independent.

When the bank began back in 1974, some four thousand women became members, paying the equivalent of less than a dollar to buy a share. Now there are nearly ten thousand active depositors, and in addition to offering savings and credit, SEWA provides supportive services like health care and legal aid.

Indira and Pushpika Freitas, two sisters who live in the Chicago area, started a program designing fabrics and fashion and sending the designs to Mumbai, where women living in slums are taught to tie-dye, block print, and sew. They make beautiful clothes that are then sold through a catalog, and 80 percent of the profits go back to the women themselves. This program too has expanded tremendously and now supports child care and health programs for the women, who are raising themselves up from conditions of dire poverty. I have known the Freitas family for a long time, and the parents are also devout and socially conscious. Even in a difficult world, we can teach our children what matters and watch with pride as they grow up to make a difference.

Making personal connections with people who are different from us is crucial to overcoming prejudice and recognizing our commonalities. I admire organizations like the Institute for International Education. Among its many programs, IIE oversees scholarships for students around the world to study in different countries. While some of their programs, such as the Fulbright fellowships, are given for advanced work, IIE also encourages college students to study internationally and gain a broader view. Allan Goodman, the distinguished professor who heads IIE, sees the broad implications of education. In the midst of the Syrian crisis, he was focused on helping the hundreds of thousands of displaced students from that country continue their education. "If we don't get to them, ISIS will," he warned.

Dr. Goodman understands on a very deep level the close connections between nonviolence and education. People who try to change the world with weapons and hate will ultimately destroy it. Those who seek change through education and understanding give us hope.

Dr. Goodman has also started programs at IIE to encourage college students to take a semester abroad, and other organizations offer programs allowing high school students to experience life in another country. Often they live with a family and attend the local school. People who have these international experiences describe them decades later as being transformative in their lives. They lived every day with a family who had different customs and traditions and outlook than they did. By sitting with them at dinner each night and celebrating holidays together, these students felt part of a bigger world. Years later, when they hear politicians decrying the dangers of immigrants or foreigners, they will have a different, broader, and much wiser perspective. Instead of being afraid of "those people," they remember fondly the exchange-year dad who cooked them dinner or the sister who walked with them under the stars.

A woman who lives in Manhattan told me about an experience she had a few years after 9/11, when the city was still reeling from the attacks. One of the pleasures of the city is the vendors who have licensed carts in even the fanciest neighborhoods, giving a small-town feel to a very big city. She worked in a glossy skyscraper in Midtown and stopped every morning to buy a banana from the fruit vendor across the street. Over many months she came to admire how hard he worked—getting up before dawn to buy his fresh fruit at the market, and then standing outside with his cart well into the night on even the coldest and hottest days. "I have two young children, and I want them to have a chance in life," he told her, explaining why he worked such long hours. They talked often, and she came to depend on his encouraging spirit to start her day. One morning he told her that the work had paid off and he was leaving for several months to return home and bring money to his family.

"Where is home?" she asked.

"Afghanistan," he said.

She jumped back as if she'd been burned and looked at him in shock. He had a heavy accent and swarthy skin, but with his kindness and good nature, she had never thought of him as the enemy. And suddenly she realized that he wasn't. She looked at his smile and felt his eagerness to see his wife and children again, and she realized he was just a man like any other, who happened to live in a dangerous country. Impulsively she gave him a hug. "Tell your family that we wish them health and happiness," she told him.

Bapuji often said, "An ounce of practice is worth more than tons of teaching." We can *talk* about understanding each other and ending bigotry, but it doesn't mean very much until we *do* something to make it happen. That might mean studying in another country or recognizing the humanity in a person who doesn't look like you (and giving him or her a hug). Most of us want the chance to have better lives for ourselves and our families and a chance to be on equal footing with others in the world. Taking action is the best way to change your own heart and influence other people's. As Bapuji put it, "Practice is the best speech and the best propaganda."

When Bapuji spoke of nonviolence, he meant much more than putting down our weapons. His focus was how to resolve a country's larger problems and inspire respect for all. As I learned on the ashram when I searched for a pencil nub in the dark of night, true nonviolence has a broadly expansive meaning. It requires us to understand the negative repercussions of waste and materialism and the positive values of treating everyone with dignity. Paying attention to only one piece of the philosophy— the absence of physical assault—can reduce the idea of nonviolence to a mockery. Those who participated in the intifada in Palestine consider themselves nonviolent because even though they pelted Israelis with stones, they didn't use guns. A group called the Ruckus Society in Berkeley, California, claims to be nonviolent because it doesn't harm people outright, though it doesn't hesitate to destroy objects and smash shop windows. This kind of behavior attracts publicity but not sympathy and understanding. You can't achieve an individual or societal transformation with baseball bats.

Our world has a long history of violence and wars and attacks by one group against another. Millions of lives have been lost to violence, and millions more have suffered from the indignities that come from bigotry and hatred. So many people throughout history were denied the good and peaceful lives they wanted. We can look back on episodes like apartheid in South Africa and know how wrong and destructive it was. Yet we find excuses for our own, equally bigoted behavior every day.

When I am frustrated by people's unwillingness to see the obvious destructiveness of their actions, I take a deep breath and remember Bapuji's calm smile. He knew that change doesn't occur quickly. The struggle for freedom and equality and peace can be long and tiring. For Bapuji, working toward an ideal meant being imprisoned many times and watching his wife and best friend die in jail.

But I think he would tell all of us now that his struggle was worthwhile, and ours will be too. A nonviolent approach to change takes time and patience. Bapuji is a reminder to all of us that equality and dignity for all is always worth fighting for—nonviolently.

The Greatest Joy

My happy memories of my grandfather were ringing in my head on the day in 2015 when a nine-foot-tall bronze statue of him was installed in Parliament Square in London. All the great leaders represented in that famous square had made major contributions to British politics and world interests.

If Bapuji were there, he would have made a joke about the statue being so much bigger than he was. And he would not have missed the irony of his statue being close to that of Sir Winston Churchill, who opposed

India's independence and was scornful of my grandfather. But Bapuji would be very proud that among all the statues of white leaders in Parliament Square, his and Nelson Mandela's statues served as symbols of how far Britain has come since the days of Churchill.

When he unveiled the statue, Prime Minister David Cameron described my grandfather as "one of the most towering figures" in political history. He was certainly towering in ideas and virtue and leadership, but he understood that at heart we are all equal. So the statue itself is closer to the ground than any of the others because my grandfather always insisted that he was one of the people.

Bapuji never saw himself as a perfect person and certainly not as a saint. He understood his own weaknesses and constantly tried to improve himself. He recognized that all the people we revere today—whether religious icons or political leaders—began as common people with common feelings. None of them was born saintly. They pushed themselves to rise above where they started.

So it makes me very sad when I hear how Bapuji's reputation is being distorted and his words misin-
terpreted in some parts of the world. At the University
of Ghana a protest by some students led to a recently
installed statue of my grandfather being taken down.
Bapuji did not live and die to be honored by statues, so
he would not have cared about that at all. But he would
have wanted to talk to the students who claimed that
he was a racist and so not worthy of being honored. As
proof, they pointed out that when he was young, he used
the word *kaffir*, now considered a derogatory term, to
describe South African blacks. I think he would have
told them that their statement is true—he did use that
word because he didn't know better and so followed
existing norms. As soon as he understood that it was
meant as a slur, he stopped using it.

He might have reminded the students that we are
not born perfect; we can only learn and try to make
ourselves better. The students complained that Bapuji
fought harder for the rights of Indians in South Africa
than for the native blacks, and they would rather have

memorials to great people of their own background. In response he might have said, "My patriotism is not an exclusive thing. . . . It is in every case, without exception, consistent with the broadest good of humanity at large." Many of the great African leaders understand that Bapuji's philosophy embraced all people. Some, like Desmond Tutu and Nelson Mandela, have cited him as a great inspiration and a role model for their own campaigns for freedom. And among African Americans, Martin Luther King praised my grandfather and followed his example of nonviolence.

Because of the controversy at the university, government officials in Ghana decided to relocate the statue to ensure its safety. They considered it a symbol of their country's friendship with India and asked people to recognize my grandfather's role "as one of the most outstanding personalities of the last century."

Other great figures from history have had their lives and actions similarly reexamined, and it's not a surprise when we find flaws in an admired hero. We make a mistake in trying to turn people into saints. We are all products of our time, of the politics and expectations of the day. Wise men like Bapuji try to take a longer and broader view and see their actions in the flow of past, present, and future.

❧❧❧

As you look at the great sweep of history, it's easy to feel insignificant and wonder what influence you can possibly have. Throughout this book I have told stories of individuals whose work has had an important impact on communities big and small because I think we can each make a difference in the lives of the people around us. You just have to care enough to try. Anybody meeting my grandfather when he was young would not have predicted that he would affect so many people and become revered as the great Mahatma Gandhi. He was skinny and small and not an obviously powerful or charismatic leader; even in his statue in Parliament Square he is dressed in his usual humble Indian garb. Whether in real life or in stone, Bapuji is a reminder that what really matters is the power of your beliefs and your willingness to pursue them.

When I was at the ashram, my grandfather was always happy to talk to me about his own frailties and foibles, and he gladly told me about his early misadventures. One of the great ambitions of his life was to erase distinctions between people and acknowledge our interdependence. When he ran the Indian Ambulance Corps during the Boer War, he risked his own life to carry the gravely injured to the field hospitals, including the Zulus who were being massacred by the British. If not for him and the Indians who volunteered alongside him, the death toll of the Zulus would have been much higher.

The scriptures of just about every religion advocate compassion, love, and respect for each other. People who don't believe in religion at all also understand those concepts as fundamental to any human interaction. Yet all of us too often forget those principles and believe only what's convenient. Real greatness comes when you can see the common humanity that we share and try to raise each other up rather than pull each other down.

We all want happiness in our lives, and we sometimes think we will find it in material things, in getting more and more at the expense of others. But happiness comes from a much deeper source. It comes from fighting for peace and justice for all people. Bapuji displayed the deep calm and contentment that all of us dream of possessing. He didn't win every struggle and he could not completely remake the world in the image that he imagined, but he remained fully engaged every day in making himself and the world better. "Joy lies in the fight, in the attempt, in the suffering involved," he said, "not in the victory itself."

Joy lies in the fight, in the attempt, in the suffering involved, not in the victory itself.

All of us can continue Bapuji's fight for peace and justice and stand firm in the power of nonviolence. I truly believe that in following my grandfather's example, we can each find for ourselves the greatest joy we are allowed on earth.

· ACKNOWLEDGMENTS ·

It certainly took more than a village to raise me, so I have to express my gratitude to everyone, starting with my grandparents and parents for showing me the value of love, compassion, and understanding. To my two sisters, Sita and Ela, who were great companions and kept me buffered between them. To my late wife, Sunanda, for giving me two wonderful children, Archana and Tushar, and the chance to practice some of the lessons learned. To my grandchildren: Dr. Paritosh Prasad, Anish Prasad, Vivan Gandhi, and finally, my one and only Princess Kasturi, who make me proud that the principles of nonviolence have successfully been transmitted to them.

Of course, without my agents Albert Lee and Jennifer Gates I wouldn't be writing this acknowledgment. They blew me away by seeing the potential of this book. The role played by my editor, Mitchell Ivers, deserves way beyond a simple thank-you. I will never be able to repay the debt of gratitude. Thank you to Kevin O'Leary for helping me build the foundation upon which this book stands. And to Janice Kaplan: I would never have been able to do this without you. You helped me find my voice on the page, and together, we are planting seeds of peace in the world.

A very big thank-you to everyone at Aevitas Creative Management, my literary agents, and Jeter Publishing, a division of Simon and Schuster, for all the assistance in making this dream come true.

This has been a labor of love and compassion, and I hope these messages will change the lives of the readers as it did my life.